About th

"*Music of the Sky*, edited by Laude & N ̣̣̣̣̣̣̣_..u, is a golden treasury of spiritual poems drawn from a variety of religious traditions and world-renowned poets. The selections are well chosen and represent religious diversity and yet reflect universal truths. If it is true that 'mystics of different religions speak the same language,' then this work proves the point. Where else would one find the great minds of the East and West brought together in a volume that can be easily read and treasured for its spiritual wealth?

"This short volume compresses the longing of the human heart and its quest for wholeness. One is led to experience such emotions as angst, hope, faith, love, and union through the words of the great mystics of the world. It forces the reader to search in the deepest corner of his/her being to truthfully confront his/her own spiritual condition. Ultimately it inspires one to find solace in the bosom of the Eternal, the Absolute, the One.

"It is a book that needs to be read, re-read, and read again and again."

—**Ishwar Harris**, the College of Wooster, and author of *The Laughing Buddha of Tofukuji: The Life of Zen Master Keido Fukushima*

"Most poets write too much for not heeding the Muse who scants her treasures. But this collection of poems come from the Muse, most definitely. Each poem threatens to spark the noetic 'Aha!' in the reader, who will see the world—and himself—suddenly from a newly enlightened perspective where the thrill of meaning and joy crystallize in deepest insight."

—**Mark Perry**, author of *On Awakening and Remembering: To Know Is to Be*

"This is a work that is sure to enchant readers who have reflected much on poetry's relation to the spirit, or ... who merely enjoy the spiritual effects of the lyrical word. These poets' words seek to remind readers of Truth, Reality, and Origin; they offer a path upon which the stones are symbols and the destination is home.... *Music of the Sky* invites us to 'repose in being'...."

—**Virginia Gray Henry**, author of *Beads of Faith*, and consulting editor for *Parabola*

World Wisdom
The Library of Perennial Philosophy

The Library of Perennial Philosophy is dedicated to the exposition of the timeless Truth underlying the diverse religions. This Truth, often referred to as the *Sophia Perennis*—or Perennial Wisdom—finds its expression in the revealed Scriptures as well as the writings of the great sages and the artistic creations of the traditional worlds.

The Perennial Philosophy provides the intellectual principles capable of explaining both the formal contradictions and the transcendent unity of the great religions.

Ranging from the writings of the great sages of the past, to the perennialist authors of our time, each series of our Library has a different focus. As a whole, they express the inner unanimity, transforming radiance, and irreplaceable values of the great spiritual traditions.

Music of the Sky: An Anthology of Spiritual Poetry appears as one of our selections in the Spiritual Classics series.

Spiritual Classics Series

This series includes szeminal, but often neglected, works of unique spiritual insight from leading religious authors of both the East and the West. Ranging from books composed in ancient India to forgotten jewels of our time, these important classics feature new introductions which place them in the perennialist context.

Cover reference: Sarasvati as goddess of poetry and music, standing on a lotus accompanied by her vehicle the swan.

Music of the Sky

An Anthology of
Spiritual Poetry

SELECTED AND EDITED BY

PATRICK LAUDE

&

BARRY MCDONALD

World Wisdom

Music of the Sky: An Anthology of Spiritual Poetry
© 2004 World Wisdom, Inc.

Most Recent Printing Indicated by last digit below:
10 9 8 7 6 5 4 3 2

Library of Congress Cataloging-in-Publication Data

Music of the sky : an anthology of spiritual poetry / selected andedited by Patrick
Laude & Barry McDonald.
p. cm. -- (Spiritual classics series)
Includes index.
ISBN 978-0-941532-45-7 (pbk. : alk. paper) 1. Religious poetry, English. 2. Religious
poetry--Translations intoEnglish. 3. Spirituality--Poetry. I. Laude, Patrick, 1958-
II.McDonald, Barry, 1952- III. Series.

PN6110.R4M87 2004
821.008'0382--dc22

2004015686.

Printed on acid-free paper in Canada

For information address World Wisdom, Inc.
P.O. Box 2682, Bloomington, Indiana 47402-2682
www.worldwisdom.com

TABLE OF CONTENTS

PART II: A GARDEN AMIDST FLAMES

PART III: THE SINGLE LIGHT

PREFACE

What do we mean when we refer to "spiritual poetry"? On the surface of things, we might say that all poems which are about God may be considered spiritual poetry, and this is true enough. Nevertheless, it seems that some additional precisions may help to clarify the subject. In the West we have settled upon the word "God" to name that Absolute Reality which is both the central object and the central subject of man's spiritual life. The anthology which you hold in your hands contains poems from many different religious traditions; this is because "sages call the One Reality by many names" (*Rig Veda*, 1.164.46) and we would not presume to limit this Reality to the province of one religious tradition. The editors of this book are at home in the Truth and Beauty which is found in the richest vein of every revelation.

Although many books have been written about the meaning of poetry, since the advent of modernism early in the last century, most students of literature are quite willing to believe that a poem can take on just about any form imaginable. From surrealism to objectivism, we have seen many literary movements come and go. In all of them experimentation is admired, and originality is prized. Words are reveled in for their own sake, and every subject becomes fair game for the poet's arrow. Even translators of the poetry written by great saints and sages of the past, such as Rumi and Mirabai, seek to recast the intense rhymes and regular meters of the originals into a language which is more in conformity with contemporary blank verse, and some of these translators have gone so far as to suggest that the most appropriate medium for spiritual poetry is found in the informal and colloquial tones of modern American English. We thank the translators for making a good deal of these spiritual writings available to a wider reading public; however, we have a very different vision of what constitutes a fully integral definition of poetry, especially "spiritual" poetry.

Apart from the content of the poem as such, the most important components of poetry are rhyme and meter. The "music" and the "rhythm" of the poem evoke what Frithjof Schuon has called "the metaphysical transparency of phenomena." Just as it is the ordering principle of the Logos which enters into manifestation and allows us to realize that God is immanent, so it is the Logos, understood as Sound and Word, which is reflected in the prosodic norms of all authentic spiritual poetry. From the perspective of traditional metaphysic, only God is Real; and it is this Reality unfolding in all of creation which permits us to see that the world is a manifestation of the Sacred. It is this underlying aspect of the deep nature of things which points to the essential function of rhyme. If God is the fundamental unity allowing for all living things to exist in harmony, then, translated into the language of poetry, God is what makes all things rhyme. This is its most profound meaning, and it explains why, since time immemorial, the formal element of rhyme has been a part of the great poetic traditions of the world; without it, the world of the poem ceases to reflect the Logos; it ceases to reflect the deep, underlying homogeneity of creation.

Similarly, in union with rhyme, we note that the role of the rhythmic component of meter also possesses an essential meaning which we may associate with the contemplative life. Understanding the heart as a symbol of the Logos in the human microcosm, we begin to realize the importance of the metrical norm in poetry: without the beating of the physical heart we cannot live; and without the prosodic "heartbeat" a poem is devoid of a rhythmic center—it loses its living pulse. The iamb, which is an unstressed followed by a stressed syllable, echoes the human heartbeat; it is one of the most ancient metrical forms, and it is as a result of the iambic meter that we are drawn into the spell of Shakespeare's sonnets. Also, it is rhythm which largely contributes to the readers' ability to interiorize the beauty of the poem; the rhythm of the poem, so to speak, allows the meaning to dance into the soul and to lodge in the memory.

The brevity of this preface does not permit us to expand further upon the critical roles of rhyme and meter in traditional poetry; however, we must underline the fact that the root of poetry is song; and being forged in music, song always contains—whether we are speaking of *bhajan* or Gregorian chant—a tonic (or key) note and a time signature. In the case of poetry, rhyme signifies the tonic note and meter signifies the time signature. In other words, the sonic and rhythmic properties of traditional poetry, which is often spiritual in nature, are essential parts of the *meaning* of the poem, and it is this part of the meaning which is sacrificed when modern translators seek to re-cast traditional poems in the more conversational idioms of contemporary free verse. As a result of these considerations, the editors have made every effort to include in this collection translations which echo something of the rhyme and rhythmical regularity of the original languages in which the poems were composed. We have also limited our short collection of poems in English to examples which reflect this norm.

If song is the root of poetry, then prayer is its flower. By prayer we mean, first of all, the deep consciousness of the Absolute. Secondly, we mean the verbal embodiment of that desire which rises from the ground of the soul and seeks to know and love the Real. The greatest examples of spiritual poetry, regardless of the individual poet's religious affiliation, reflect a knowledge of God which has become so ingrained in the substance of the poet's soul that when he opens his mouth to speak, flowers bloom in every word. The verbal art of the spiritual poem is meant to serve its meaning, which inevitably centers on God. If the role of art is to reflect Truth and Beauty, and to nourish that which is best in man, then the final goal of art must concern God; for the man who sees through the *maya* of the here-below, God is the only Subject which finally matters.

The selections chosen for *Music of the Sky* range over an enormous geography, and they were written by men and women representing many different religious traditions; however, they all have, as their primary reference, that spiritual Reality which has the power to transform and illuminate our subjectivity. The gift of each poem resides in the magical quality of the language to communicate some spark of that illumination from soul to soul. Many of the poems in this anthology were written by saints, and they are thus windows into brilliantly illuminated souls. Each individual poem, and the entire book itself, is meant to be a kind of viaticum; something to carry on a journey, regardless of whether the journey is viewed horizontally across a vast stretch of space, or vertically as an ascent into the highest realms of thought. Rather than attempting to provide a volume which professes to be a definitive collection, this book simply presents a spreading fan of poems, each of which is like a candle in the dark.

Barry McDonald

INTRODUCTION

At its best poetry is indeed a "music of the sky." Poets are the first to claim a musical quality for their words, as elusive and ill-defined as this quality may remain. Essentially, music has been defined as the art of the arrangement of sounds, both horizontally—in a melody—, and vertically—through harmonies. Plato defined philosophy as "the noblest and best of music"[1] which amounts to saying that music can be understood to deal with realities other than sounds and, more generally, that it can focus on the arrangement of parts into a whole. Music is the art of Apollo whose name means, according to the self-same Plato, "'moving together,' whether in the poles of heaven as they are called, or in the harmony of song, which is termed concord, because he moves all together by an harmonious power, as astronomers and musicians ingeniously declare. And he is the God who presides over harmony, and makes all things move together (*homopolon*), both among Gods and among men."[2] From such an understanding, one can derive a definition of music as the art of "moving together," an art that poetry exercises in the realm of words, those precious encounters of sound and meaning.

As for the sky (in the Platonic sense): it spans the upper realm of the archetypes, the essential forms that are the paradigmatic principles of physical realities. In the wake of scientistic phenomenism and materialism, this doctrine has come to be understood by most modern readers as an "abstraction"; so much so that the archetype is considered as, at best, no more than a universal concept or an ideal of reason—when it is not reduced to a chaotic protoplasm in the depths of the inferior psyche. Still, any vision of the world that recognizes the primacy of a spiritual

---

[1] *Phaedo*, 60e (Benjamin Jowett trans.).
[2] *Cratylus*, 404d (Benjamin Jowett trans.).

1

Substance must admit, in one way or another, that physical realities cannot but proceed from invisible and essential patterns of being. The doctrine of creation *ex nihilo* itself presupposes that phenomenal realities—the "more" of creation—cannot proceed from a "lesser" reality since they reach the shore of existence in a state of being that is already perfected. Even the *nihil* of monotheism does not preclude "ideas" in the creative Word of God, since this term may be taken to mean "no-thing" in the sense of "no created thing." The highest poetry testifies to this realm of ideas. The powerful emotional effect that it can have on us is the best evidence of its touching inner strings that have been tuned on high.

*
* *

The connection between poetry and spiritual contemplation has been highlighted on many accounts and in many ways, so much so that it has become a sort of truism. In common parlance, the poet is often considered as an intuitive and meditative soul who enjoys a rare ability to contemplate reality in a more profound and subtle way than do most fellow human beings. Accordingly, one often deems poets to be endowed with a mediumistic ability that somehow allows them to gain access into the deepest layers of reality. By virtue of this ability, the poet was traditionally conceived as a mediator or a channel between the essence of things and the magic of words, crystallizing his perceptions into sounds and images that pierce through the veil of trivial usage and bring miracles out of language. However, the idea of poetic contemplation covers a wide spectrum of phenomena, and while all genuine poetry is in a sense "contemplative" it does not follow that the discipline of spiritual practice necessarily enters into the alchemy of poetic creation; hence the need to specify the scope of our anthology.

In the Christian spiritual tradition, contemplation has often been defined in contradistinction to the reading of Scriptures (*lectio divina*), meditation, and the practice of vocal prayer.

The latter is most often envisaged as a personal, volitional and sentimental motion of the soul directed towards God. By contrast, meditation involves the discursive process of reason, even though this discourse may be accompanied by the evocation of images and ultimately results in emotional affects, as in the practice of Ignatian meditation. In contemplation, as suggested by the prefix "con-," motion and discourse are somehow superseded by a synthetic, immediate and inarticulate mode of being—not mere thinking—that entails both totality and centering. Spiritual contemplation engages our entire being while rooting it in the unshakable ground of the Divine; it suggests union with the One, and therefore Self-sufficiency and repose in Being.

By contrast with this self-contained and synthetic character of contemplation, poetry always implies, by definition, the idea of a production—poems or *poemata*. Etymologically speaking, the Greek word *poiesis* literally means "creation," and specifically refers to creation in the realm of the *logos*. Although the scope of the term *logos* has tended to become more and more limited to the plane of rationality, its original meaning remains far from being exhausted by its reference to the realm of the discursive mind. The etymology of the Greek word suggests the idea of a gathering or a collecting, thereby alluding to the distillation of a unity of understanding and discourse out of a multiplicity of perceptions.

In Christianity, the *Logos* was understood in the context of the Incarnation; it was therefore identified with Christ as the Divine and human manifestation of the redeeming Truth. In this context, the Word might best be defined as the perfection and prototype of Creation in God—the Model for all things, so to speak—while being also, from another standpoint, the perfection and culmination of Creation in man; hence the central position of mankind in the universe, a position that is symbolized, in the Bible, by the human privilege of naming creatures.[3] The human ability to "name" beings clearly pertains to the Word as point of

---

[3] Genesis, 2:19-20.

junction between the Divine and the human. The *Logos* is the nexus between these two realms, and thus the means of communication *par excellence* between the two; it is both divine Revelation and human Invocation. In the first case, God speaks in a human language as it were, while man's prayer is most fundamentally a divine idiom. From the standpoint of the "descent" into being, the "poetic" Act of God through His Word is Creation, whereas in the perspective of the "ascent" toward God, this Act is to be understood as the theomorphic and deifying Norm[4] and the Way back to God. As is most directly expressed by the prologue of St. John's Gospel, God creates through His Word:

> *In principio erat Verbum,*
> *Et Verbum erat apud Deum,*
> *Et Deus erat Verbum.*
> *Hoc erat in principio apud Deum.*
> *Omnia per ipsum facta sunt:*
> *Et sine ipso factum est nihil, quod factum est.*[5]

Mankind, in his universal aspect, therefore constitutes the Divine "Poem" *par excellence*, and as such the prototype of the whole Creation.

In India, the sacred syllable *Omkara*, as a quintessence of Divine Revelation, constitutes the essence of all poetry. Similarly, in Islam, the Quran is the divine Revelation, and the divine Name *Allah* is—for the Sufis—the synthesis of the Book. Kabbalists tend

---

[4] Hence the Catholic idea of the "imitation of Christ" (*Imitatio Christi*).

[5] "In the beginning was the Word, and the Word was with God, and the Word was God. The same was in the beginning with God. All things were made by him; and without him was not any thing made that was made" (John, 1:1-3). As presented in St. John's prologue, the relationship between *Deus* and *Verbum* is what Ananda Coomaraswamy proposed to define as a "distinction without difference." This expression is Coomaraswamy's translation for the Sanskrit *bhedabheda*. It is implied by the double function of *Verbum* as substantive "predicate" of *Deus* and as object of the preposition *apud* ("with": in the sense of abiding by). God is "no different" from His Word since the Word is, so to speak, the irradiation of God; but He is "distinct" from His Word in so far as the Word is the Prototype of Relativity.

to endow the Names of God with the same synthetic power. Each in its way could be viewed as the quintessence of poetry.

The point of view of Far Eastern traditions is somewhat different in that they do not stem from Revelation as a Book or as an Original Utterance. In the Chinese and Japanese traditions—by virtue of the shamanistic roots of Taoism, Confucianism and Shinto—the word or the book is Nature, or it is synthesized by the fundamental "signatures" that are the combination of cosmic principles, *yin* and *yang*, as manifested first and foremost in the *I Ching*. It could be said that these traditions do not consider poetry as a prolongation of the verbal irruption of the Supreme in the world, but rather, that they envisage poetical creation as a mode of conformity to the immanent "traces" of the Divine in Nature.

*

* *

Whether one considers the Divine Word as expressed through Revelation and Scripture, or as manifested in the Book of Nature, the human poet is but an imitator of the Divine Poet; in non-theistic parlance, it could be said that he is "attuned" to the productive Way of the Principle, since his "logical" (stemming from the *logos*) utterance is simultaneously a "poetical" work (referring here to *poiesis* as creation or "making"). In their original root, "poetry" and "logic" are one and the same.[6] It is through a profound attention to this reality that Emerson associated the Son of the Christian Trinity with the Sayer and with Beauty (the Father corresponding to the Knower and the True, and the Spirit to the Good and the Doer); whence his elliptical formula: "Beauty is the creator of the universe." The Son is the Perfection of Creation

---

[6] "According to traditional doctrines, logic and poetry have a common source, the Intellect, and far from being contradictory are essentially complementary. Logic becomes opposed to poetry only if respect for logic becomes transformed into rationalism, and poetry, rather than being a vehicle for the expression of a truly intellectual knowledge, becomes reduced to sentimentalism or a means of expressing individual idiosyncrasies and forms of subjectivism" (Seyyed Hossein Nasr, *Islamic Art and Spirituality* [Albany, New York, 1987], p.91).

and He is also its Door. Beauty is the Hidden Perfection of God from which all things are created. In its essence, or at its height, poetry is accordingly the echo of the Divine Logos.

Poetry may thus be understood as the essence of language; or it could also be said that the very root of language was—or is—poetry, before any distinction between poetry and prose be drawn. Every word, therefore, virtually partakes of poetry, even before being used in a line or a sentence, because every word is a symbolic treasury of virtually limitless implications. Whence flows Emerson's reminder concerning the synthetic character of poetry: "It does not need that a poem should be long. Every word was once a poem." And there is little doubt that when Mallarmé proposed to "give a purer meaning to the words of the tribe" (*donner un sens plus pur aux mots de la tribu*), he had some intuition of this original poetic vibration of the word, particularly of its root. The primordial power of this radical vibration—in which the auditory and semantic dimensions are as it were fused together—explains why poets are in fact the keepers of the symbolic richness of words. They both "attend to" the integrity of language and "open" it by unveiling the limitless potentialities of its foundations.

In all spiritual traditions, we find the idea that language was originally much richer and more synthetic than it is today. Language has tended to become reduced to its practical and communicative dimension—be it purely social or idiosyncratic— whereas its essence is actually symbolic. In other words, poetry is not only a means of communication with others and an expression of oneself; it is also—and above all—a way for transcendent Reality to manifest itself in and through words, images and music. By virtue of this symbolic power not only to represent and communicate, but also to make present, it is fundamentally polysemic: it offers multiple strata of meaning and cannot be reduced to the single horizontal dimension of conceptual communication. This virtually unlimited multiplicity of meanings—unlimited in proportion to the depth of the poetry—must not however be confused with the relativistic claim that reduces poetry to a matter of subjective readings in the name of hermeneutic freedom. The very partial merit of this relativistic claim lies in the emphasis it places upon the individual as a locus of actualization of meaning. However, the "making" sense of the poem is not only a matter of subjective actuation; it is also—and primarily—one of objective and essential potency. Metaphysically speaking, one must maintain the radical objectivity and ontological power of the word both as shaktic or "magic" reality and as pure potentiality. In this sense, the Word is the very act of Being.

As a way of access to the primordial richness of language, poetry is deeply connected to memory and anamnesis—memory being understood here in its profound and quasi-timeless connection with truth, and not simply as a psychic repository of ideas and images. Ananda Coomaraswamy has emphasized the fact that traditional literature—before the advent of modernity—was exclusively poetic: "Ours is a prose style, while the traditional lore of all peoples—even the substance of their practical sciences—has been everywhere poetical." By contrast, the modern and contemporary disjunction between the intellective dimension of "logic" and the domain of poetry testifies to a desacralization of knowledge on the one hand, and to a debasement of poetry on the other hand. It is one of the major symptoms of what Gilbert Durand has proposed to call the "schizomorphic" sickness of modern man, i.e. the fragmentation of inner and outer reality that results in disintegration and irreconcilable oppositions.

In many cosmogonies, the process of creation is presented as an encounter between two complementary principles that are both necessary in order for the world to be. The Bible tells us that "the Spirit of God was hovering over the waters"[7] whereas Hindu cosmology refers to *Purusha* and *Prakriti* as the two principles of manifestation. The first of these principles is active, determinative and "informing" while the second is plastic and receptive. Analogously, the poetical work tends to be conceived as the outcome of the encounter between "form" (*idea* or *eidos*, intelligible principle) and "matter" (*hyle*, substantial or hypostatic

---

[7] Genesis, 1:2.

principle), or "meaning" and "form" (taken this time in the ordinary sense of the word). We find the same complementary pair of creative principles—with different emphases and nuances—in all major poetics, and the harmonic coincidence of the two elements involved is always understood as being brought about by the clear subordination of the substratum in relation to the intellective form.[8] This "crystallization" of the coincidence between intellective essence and linguistic substance is primarily effected through meter. As God "disposes everything according to measure, number, and weight" (*omnia in mensura, numero et pondere disposuisti*),[9] as He manifests the world through the qualitative measures of cosmic order, the poet analogously creates by manifesting the *eidos*, the spiritual meaning, within the domain of linguistic substance and through meter. In other words, the form is as if absorbed by the essence through the prosodic number. The latter is the very mode of poetic creation. It is not an arbitrary constraint but the expression of quality and intelligibility within the realm of quantity.[10] Number is the prototype of measure and is therefore the manifesting and ordering principle of creation, the poem.[11]

In so far as number and measure are none other than expressions of unity, they also constitute the essence of rhythm as

---

[8] As Ray Livingston articulates the matter: "The universe itself, properly viewed by the Intellect, or the 'eye of the heart,' as it is often called, is the result of the marriage of Harmony (*saman*) and the Word (*rc*) or, in another idiom, the union of essence and substance.... When there is a true union of those principles, the result is 'an effective harmony and the reproduction of the higher of the two principles involved.'" (*The Traditional Theory of Literature* [Minneapolis, 1962], p.77).

[9] Wisdom of Solomon, 11:20.

[10] In René Guénon's words: "It can be said that the relation of measure to number corresponds, in an inversely analogical sense, to the relation of manifestation to its essential principle" (*The Reign of Quantity & the Signs of the Times* [Ghent, New York, 1995], pp.36-7).

[11] "Number, gentlemen, number! Or else order and symmetry; for order is nothing else than ordered number, and symmetry is nothing but perceived and compared order" (Joseph de Maistre, *Les soirées de Saint-Petersbourg* [Paris, 1821], 2:125).

the "formal" pole of poetry. Rhythm, which plays such a central role in contemplative meditation and methods of invocation, must be understood as the expression of Unity within multiplicity; it is the very "vibration" of the One. In and through it the "other" participates in the "Same." In this connection, rhythm is closely associated with incantation as a spiritual method of return to the One. Through rhythm, the One makes itself present in multiplicity, the Formless inhabits form: rhythm is the *barzakh* (the intermediary zone) between the instant of eternity and temporal sequence. From an animic standpoint, the mobility and perpetual "otherness" of the soul may be integrated by means of the "sameness" of the recurring patterns brought out by rhythmic practice. As Ananda Coomaraswamy has pointed out, the "singsong" reading of sacred texts is none other than the "performing" aspect of this rhythmic law. Monotony and absence of psychic expressiveness is a direct manifestation of the spiritual grounding of sacred chant in the One. This principle is central in sacred and liturgical psalmody, as is testified to by authentic Gregorian chant and traditional Quranic recitation. It is important to keep in mind, in this connection, that poetry should be read aloud, preferably sung. Poetry is not only a manifestation within the realm of multiplicity, it is also an exteriorization; and singing is the very symbol and means of this exteriorization. In this context, it should be recalled that the sacred text—essence or epitome of all poetical works, and always eminently poetic itself, as is the Quran in the context of the Arabic language—proceeds by what Frithjof Schuon has characterized as a kind of "ruse."[12] It makes use of multiplicity and exteriorization in order to bring

---

[12] "Like the world, the Quran is at the same time one and multiple. The world is a multiplicity which disperses and divides; the Quran is a multiplicity which draws together and leads to Unity. The multiplicity of the holy Book—the diversity of its words, aphorisms, images and stories—fills the soul, and then absorbs it and imperceptibly transposes it into a climate of serenity and immutability by a sort of 'divine ruse.' The soul, which is accustomed to the flux of phenomena, yields to this flux without resistance; it lives in phenomena and is by them divided and dispersed—even more than that, it actually becomes what it thinks and does. The revealed Discourse has the virtue of accepting

back the ten thousand things to the One. This is what could be called the alchemy of diversity. Accordingly, rhythm functions both as an expression of the One and as a necessity stemming from the spiritual and intellectual structure of our being. As a reflection of the *Logos* it is the ebb and flow of Reality.

On the "substantial" plane of "words" rhythm, or meter, is like the imprint of the One; and it could be said, in this connection, that through rhythm, meter, or prosody, form participates in the essence. On the highest level, the essence is to be understood as the ineffable Principle—since God is the meaning of everything— the vibrant Silence that is the alpha and the omega of all poetry and all music, of all worlds. However, we must also consider the relationship between essence and form from the standpoint of "meaning" or "content." The latter is always considered as more determinative or as ultimately more "real" than the formal structure.[13]

In Japanese poetry, for example, the *haiku* must fulfill some "formal" requirements that pertain to rhythm, as well as to the lexicon, but it cannot be a *haiku* without integrating an "essential" element, the *hai-i*, the *haiku* spirit.[14] Similarly, Hindu poetics entirely revolves around the notion of *rasa* or "taste," a notion that evokes the divine and beatific infinitude as it is experienced

this tendency while reversing its movement thanks to the celestial character of the content and the language, so that the fishes of the soul swim without distrust and with their habitual rhythm into the divine net" (*Understanding Islam* [Bloomington, IN, World Wisdom, 1998], pp.47-8).

[13] As Ray Livingston points out: "The letter or sound is the outward aspect which is of little importance compared to the spirit or meaning embodied in the words" (*The Traditional Theory of Literature*, p.78).

[14] "... *Haiku* as a 17 syllabled verse is formally similar to the upper strophe of *waka*, except that every *haiku* must have *kigo* (season-word). However, the mere fulfillment of this formal requirement does not necessarily produce a *haiku*, if it is devoid of *hai-i* (haiku spirit), as is often the case. A verse of 17 syllabled words with the inner division of 5/7/5 without *hai-i*, even if it is provided with *kigo* (season-word), would not make a *haiku*; it could at the very most make an imperfect *waka*. That which makes a *haiku* genuinely *haiku* is not its formal structure but rather the *hai-i*, the *haiku* spirit" (Toshihiko and Toyo Izutsu, *The Theory of Beauty in the Classical Aesthetics of Japan* [The Hague, 1981], pp.64-5).

by and through the Self.[15] It is a participation in the music of the Infinite.

Now such terms as *hai-i* or *rasa* refer to a somewhat "ineffable" and "indefinite" reality—although they may give rise to very specific descriptions and classifications in terms of their modalities—precisely because they pertain to Infinitude, as expressed in the Hindu concept of *ananda* or, in a different way and in Japanese parlance, in the term *fueki*, the "metaphysical ground," "non-articulated wholeness" (Izutsu), or Naught.[16] On whatever level and in whatever mode one may consider it, this infinite (opening onto the Boundless) and indefinite (that cannot be caught in the net of concepts and words) Reality is the end (in both senses of *telos* and limit) and the essence of poetry, but it is also transcendent in relation to the poem as a formal structure. Here the analogy between the poem and the human subject allows for a clearer understanding of the relation between "essence" and "form": in Hindu terms, just as *Atman* is both transcendent and immanent in relation to the individual self, the "spirit of the poem" is both the very principle of the poem as well as being something situated beyond the poem as a formal entity. If poetry cannot be easily defined, it is not because it is vague or purely subjective, but because it is situated at the junction between form and essence, and opens onto the Infinite.

To put the matter in a paradoxical way, poetry "has something to say" which "cannot be said." It "has something to say": it may not always be didactic, but it is still, if genuine, the result of a kind of necessity, the outcome of a pressure or a need to crystallize a "meaning" into a "form." A contemporary poet such as Rainer Maria Rilke was still very keenly aware of this urgent

---

[15] "The savor is the essence, the 'self' (*atman*) of the poem ... According to the *Agni Purana*, savor is derived from the third form of the tri-unity in its metaphysical aspect, *sat-chit-ananda*, 'being-consciousness-bliss,' through the intermediary of the 'self' and pleasure in general" (René Daumal, *Rasa or Knowledge of the Self* [New York, 1982], p.105).

[16] *Fueki* refers to the intrinsic nature of the infinite Void whereas *ananda* suggests the dynamic power of the infinite Self.

and necessary character of poetry—the best name for which is inspiration—when he wrote to a would-be poet:

> This most of all: ask yourself in the most silent hour of the night: *must* I write? Dig into yourself for a deep answer. And if the answer rings out in assent, if you meet this solemn question with a strong, simple "I must," then build your life in accordance with this necessity.[17]

Poetry is "given to," or rather, "imparted upon" the poet, whether it has the crystalline brevity of *haiku* or the powerful grandeur and length of the epic.[18] This is the inspiration from the "gods" or from the "muses" that the twentieth-century surrealists caricatured with their "automatic writing," confusing the light of the super-conscious with the darkness and chaos of the sub-conscious. Being literally "in-spired," true poetry is therefore a rare occurrence, especially in times of spiritual scarcity such as ours.

"Which cannot be said": poetry is akin to experience, or let us say to presence. Poetry is the articulation of a contemplative perception. It is the result of an encounter between a subject and an object, and ultimately the verbal crystallization of an identification between them. In the modern world, poetry is often conceived as "subjective" and purely "emotional" because of a misunderstanding or an abuse of this principle. Normatively, poetry is the crystallization of what Daumal quite suggestively

---

[17] *Letters to a Young Poet* (New York, 1987), p.6.

[18] As Seyyed Hossein Nasr comments on one of the masterpieces of Sufi poetry: "Shaykh Mahmud Shabistari, the author of the *Gulshan-i raz* (*The Secret Rose Garden*), which is one of the greatest masterpieces of Persian Sufi poetry, writes: 'Everyone knows that during all my life, I have never intended to compose poetry. Although my temperament was capable of it, rarely did I choose to write poems.' Yet in spite of himself, Shabistari, in a period of a few days, and through direct inspiration (*ilham*) composed one of the most enduring and widely read poetical masterpieces of Oriental literature. Moreover, he composed in perfect rhyming couplets and the *mathnawi* meter while remaining oblivious to the canons of prosody as contained in the classical works on the subject" (*Islamic Art and Spirituality*, pp.93-4).

calls "an objective emotion." Objective in the sense that it is grounded in an archetype—the essence of a phenomenon or a perception; and emotional in the sense that the soul reacts to this archetype in which she recognizes, more or less clearly, her very substance. In this way, a sentiment can be quite objective, and certainly more so than an ineffective reason severed from its intellective and intuitive root.

Let us consider Japanese *haiku* as an example: in it, the subject participates in the very mode of nature's operations. The poem is like a glimpse into the emergence of the Whole, of the Infinite, into a given form, a given ambience. In a sense, *haiku* constitutes a limit of poetry since, with it, language is reduced to its minimal manifestation, in order to suggest the full Reality of That from which the phenomenon emerges. In this regard, poetry must suggest the very ineffability of the object that it attempts to convey. It is a form of the Formless. Baudelaire had an intuition of this function of poetry when he defined it as a capacity to recover childhood and perceive a given phenomenon "in all its freshness, as the very symbol of reality." One could say of the true *haiku* what Titus Burckhardt so suggestively wrote of Far-Eastern landscape painting:

> In paintings of landscapes of a Buddhist inspiration (*ch'an*), all the elements, mountains, trees and clouds, are present only to mark, in contrast, the void from which they seem to spring forth in this very instant and against which they detach themselves as ephemeral islands.[19]

Of course, not all poetry must conform to this "minimalist" pattern. However, even the most expanded plenitude of expression, if truly poetic, tends to resonate with contemplative Silence—that vibrant essence which is none other than the Heart as source of all songs.

*

* *

[19] *Sacred Art in East and West* (Bloomington, IN, World Wisdom/Louisville, KY, Fons Vitae, 2001), pp.183-4.

Because it results from an encounter between form and essence, poetry as such cannot be translated. Poems may be translated of course, but it will always be at the expense of that dimension of poetry that is not reducible to meaning. This does not amount to saying that translations cannot convey some of the beauty of the original. In fact, there are many images which can be translated without losing their symbolic impact. Indeed, a large majority of the poems included in *Music of the Sky* were written in a language other than English. The inclusion of original texts, however, was precluded by the intended size of the volume. The benefit and enjoyment of the few readers who would have been able to read some of the poems in this or that language had to be sacrificed to a more general purpose. At any rate, the few English poems that are the exceptions to the rule will continue to suggest to the reader the importance of metrical rhythm and harmony. Prosody is not just a constraint; it has its roots in one of the deepest needs of our mind and soul.

Music of the Sky has been conceived as a *vade mecum*, not as an anthology aiming at any kind of exhaustiveness or near perfect representativeness. The reader should be able to open it at any page, at any time, in virtually any situation, traveling or enjoying a moment of contemplative rest. The organization of the various pieces into three categories is general and flexible enough to adjust to this type of happy and discontinuous reading, while suggesting the three planes of all spiritual life: fear, rigor and separation; love, mercy and union; knowledge and unity. There is something in us that must die; there is something in us that must live; there is something in us that wants to know and to be. Or else, "hatred of the world, love of God; but there is a degree which exceeds both of these and this is certainty of the Real."[20]

Patrick Laude

[20] Frithjof Schuon, *Logic and Transcendence* (London, 1975), p.163.

Part I

Dust
from
the
Whirlwind

Song of the Ghost Dance

The wind stirs the willows
The wind stirs the willows
The wind stirs the grasses
The wind stirs the grasses

Fog! Fog!
Lightning! Lightning!
Whirlwind! Whirlwind!

The whirlwind!
The whirlwind!
The snowy earth comes gliding
The snowy earth comes gliding.

There is dust from the whirlwind.
There is dust from the whirlwind.
The whirlwind on the mountain,
The whirlwind on the mountain.
The rocks are ringing,
The rocks are ringing.
They are ringing in the mountains,
They are ringing in the mountains.

—Paiute, *American Indian Poetry: An Anthology of Songs and Chants* by
George W. Cronyn (New York, 1962)

Nothing lives long
Nothing lives long
Nothing lives long
Except the earth and the mountains.

—Cheyenne, *The Magic World: American Indian Songs and Poems* by
William Brandon (New York, 1971)

What is life?
It is the flash of a firefly in the night;
It is the breath of a buffalo in the winter time;
It is the little shadow that runs across the grass
And loses itself in the sunset.

—Chief Isapwo Muksika Crowfoot, *Studies in Comparative Religion*
(Winter–Spring, 1979)

You and I shall Go

It is above that you and I shall go;
Along the Milky Way you and I shall go;
Along the flower trail you and I shall go;
Picking flowers on our way you and I shall go.

—Wintu, *In the Trail of the Wind: American Indian Poems and Ritual Orations*
by John Bierhorst (New York, 1971)

All doctrines split asunder
Zen teaching cast away—
Four score years and one.
The sky now cracks and falls
The earth cleaves open—
In the heart of the fire
Lies a hidden spring.

—Giun, *Japanese Death Poems* by Yoel Hoffman (Tokyo, 1986)

Seventy-one!
How did
a dewdrop last?

—Kigen, *Japanese Death Poems* by Yoel Hoffman (Tokyo, 1986)

Empty-handed I entered the world
Barefoot I leave it.
My coming, my going—
Two simple happenings
That got entangled.

—Kozan Ichikyo, *Japanese Death Poems* by Yoel Hoffman (Tokyo, 1986)

The pure morning dew
Has no use for this world.

—Issa, *The Moon in the Pines* selected and translated by Jonathan Clements
(New York, 2000)

Story on story of wonderful hills and stream,
Their blue-green haze locked in clouds!
Mists brush my thin cap with moisture,
Dew wets my coat of plaited straw.
On my feet I wear pilgrim's sandals,
My hand holds a stick of old rattan.
Though I look down again on the dusty world,
What is that land of dreams to me?

—Han Shan, *Cold Mountain: 100 Poems by the T'ang Poet Han Shan*
translated by Burton Watson (New York, 1970)

Walking along a narrow path at the foot of a mountain
I come to an ancient cemetery filled with countless
    tombstones
And thousand-year-old oaks and pines.
The day is ending with a lonely, plaintive wind.
The names on the tombs are completely faded,
And even the relatives have forgotten who they were.
Choked with tears, unable to speak,
I take my staff and return home.

—Ryokan, *One Robe, One Bowl: The Zen Poetry of Ryokan* translated by
John Stevens in *Buddhadharma: The Practioner's Quarterly* (Winter, 2002)

Eternal spring wind,
I know you won't be too rough
On the delicate
Branches and buds
Of the weeping willow.

—Rengetsu, *Lotus Moon: The Poetry of the Buddhist Nun Rengetsu*
translated by John Stevens (New York, 1994)

Why bother with the world?
Let others go gray, bustling east, west.
In this mountain temple, lying half-in,
Half-out,
I'm removed from joy and sorrow.

—Ryushu, *Zen Prayers, Sermons, Anecdotes, Interviews* translated by Lucien
Stryk and Takashi Ikemoto (New York, 1963)

A dash of rain upon
The lotus leaves. But the leaves
Remain unmarked, no matter
How hard the raindrops beat.
Mind, be like the lotus leaves,
Unstained by the world.

—Chong Ch'ol, *Anthology of Korean Literature from Early Times to the Nineteenth Century* compiled and edited by Peter H. Lee (Honolulu, 1981)

By the highway of Release I came,
Yet by the highway I did not go.
Stumbling on the crazy bridge of fame,
Lost I my day, for I did not know.
Falling to the stream of death, I found
Naught in my mind for the ferry fee:
Not a cowry though I looked around,
Nor the name of Hari for saving me.
Birth in womb of woman thus for me
No more availed than an empty dream.
Birth from woman also is for thee:
Gain then Knowledge of the Self-Supreme.

—Lalla Yogishwari, *The Word of Lalla* translated by Sir Richard Temple
(Cambridge, UK, 1924)

Mother! Mother! My boat sinks in the ocean of this world:
Fiercely the hurricane of delusion rages on all sides!
The mind is my clumsy helmsman: stubborn passions, my six
    oarsmen:
I sailed my boat into a pitiless wind
I sailed my boat, and now it is sinking!
The rudder of devotion is split: tattered is the sail of faith:
Into my boat the waters pour! Tell me now, what shall I do?
With failing eyes, alas! I see nothing but darkness—
Here in the waves I must swim,
O Mother, and cling to the raft of Thy name!

    —Bengali Hymn, *A Treasury of Traditional Wisdom* presented by Whitall N.
                                Perry (Louisville, 1992)

Because Thou lovest the Burning-ground,
I have made a Burning-ground of my heart—
That Thou, Dark One, who haunts the Burning-ground,
Mayest dance Thy eternal dance.
Nothing else is in my heart, O Mother:
Day and night blazed the funeral pyre:
The ashes of the dead, strewn all about,
I have preserved against Thy coming;
With death-conquering Mahakala neath Thy feet
Enter Thou in, dancing Thy rhythmic dance,
That I may behold Thee with closed eyes.

> —Bengali Hymn to Kali, *A Treasury of Traditional Wisdom* presented by
> Whitall N. Perry (Louisville, 1992)

O mother, I have fallen in love
With the Beautiful One—He knows
No death; He knows no decay and has no form.

I have fallen in love, O mother,
With the Beautiful One—He has no middle
And no end; He has no parts and no features.

O mother, I have fallen in love
With the Beautiful One—He knows no birth
And he has no fear.

I have fallen in love with the Beautiful One—
He is without a family, without country,
And He is without peer—
Chenna Mallikarjuna, the Beautiful, is my husband.
Fling into fire husbands subject to death and to decay.

—Akka Mahadevi, *A Treasury of Traditional Wisdom* presented by Whitall N.
Perry (Louisville, 1992)

You are kind, I am the pitiable one,
You are the donor, I am the beggar,
I am the notorious sinner, You are the destroyer of accumulated sins,
You are the master, I am the orphan, who is orphaned like me?
There is no one afflicted like me, and no one like you to
    destroy affliction,
You are the Supreme Self, I am the individual soul,
Father, Mother, Teacher, Friend, you are my helper in all ways.
Between you and me there are so many relationships.
Whatever Tulsi feels, you are that,
O! Compassionate One! I seek refuge at your feet,
O! Lord! If you are the One who showers mercy on the poor,
    then
I am the poor one.

—Tulsidas, *Sacred Songs of India* by V.K. Subramanian (New Delhi, 1996)

Guide this little boat
over the waters,
what can I give you for fare?
Our mutable world holds nothing but grief,
bear me away from it.
Eight bonds of karma
have gripped me—
the whole of creation
swirls through eight million wombs,
through eight million birth-forms we flicker.
Mira cries: Dark One—
take this little boat to the far shore,
put an end to coming
and going.

—Mirabai, *For Love of the Dark One: Songs of Mirabai* translated by Andrew
Schelling (Boston, 1993)

Don't let go, hold on tight,
　And win through, my dear.
All night's darkness is in flight.
　Gone is all your fear.
Look above—on the East's face,
Over the deepest forest-place,
The morning star has risen clear.
　Gone is all your fear.

These are marauders of the night:
　Self-doubt, the skeptic's sneer,
Dejection, sloth. At dawn's light
　See them disappear.
Come outside, come quickly, fly—
Look up, look up and see—the sky
Is full of light and bright and sheer.
　Gone is all your fear.

—Rabindranath Tagore, *Song Offerings* translated by Joe Winter
(London, 2000)

O now beneath your feet's dust let
  My head kneel on the ground.
Yield up my arrogance to tears,
  Let all my pride be drowned.
If glory to myself I offer
It is self-insult that I suffer—
And then I die within myself,
  Turning around, around.
Yield up my arrogance to tears,
  Let all my pride be drowned.

Let me not advertise myself
  In various things I do—
But let my deeds fit your desire,
  That your will may come through.
O for your true peace is my longing,
And your dear image's belonging.
Within my heart of lotus petal
  May your shield be found.
Yield up my arrogance to tears,
  Let all my pride be drowned.

—Rabindranath Tagore, *Song Offerings* translated by Joe Winter
(London, 2000)

How many in this life can never
wash away all their sins
and must live, alas, in vain,
for they remain unaware.
How many remain blindfolded
by their own fecklessness,
never wasting even a crust
on the true path of God.

This world is a newly wed bride
adorned in green and red:
each one in turn gazes on her
and never wearies of it.

How many lions are thus
carried away by death.
Of Azraël, Death's angel,
None can resist the claws.

And now, Yunus, you too
must strip yourself bare on your path.
Should a hundred armed men come,
they cannot rob a naked man.

—Yunus Emre, *Yunus Emre: The Wandering Fool* translated by Edouard
Roditi (San Francisco, 1987)

If thou canst walk on water
Thou art no better than a straw.
If thou canst fly into the air
Thou art no better than a fly.
Conquer thy heart
That thou mayest become somebody.

—Ansari, *A Treasury of Traditional Wisdom* presented by Whitall N. Perry
(Louisville, 1992)

I died as mineral and became a plant,
I died as plant and rose to animal,
I died as animal and I was Man.
Why should I fear? When was I less by dying?
Yet once more I shall die as Man, to soar
With angels blest; but even from angelhood
I must pass on: *all except God doth perish.*
When I have sacrificed my angel-soul,
I shall become what no mind e'er conceived.
Oh, let me not exist! For Non-existence
Proclaims in organ tones: "To Him we shall return."

—Rumi, *Rumi: Poet and Mystic* translated by Reynold A. Nicholson
(London, 1950)

"Needs must I tear them out," the peacock cried,
"These gorgeous plumes which only tempt my pride?"

Of all his talents let the fool beware:
Mad for the bait, he never sees the snare.
Harness to fear of God thy strength and skill,
Else there's no bane so deadly as free-will.

—Rumi, *Rumi: Poet and Mystic* translated by Reynold A. Nicholson
(London, 1950)

Old tent-maker, your body is a tent,
Your soul a sultan from the eternal world.
Death's messenger gives the call to journey on,
And strikes the tent, and lets the sultan go.

—Omar Khayyam, translated from the Persian by L.P. Elwell-Sutton in *In Search of Omar Khayyam* by Ali Dashti (New York, 1971)

Last night I dropped and smashed my porcelain bowl,
A clumsy folly in a bout of drinking.
The shattered bowl in dumb appeal cried out,
"I was like you, you too will be like me."

—Omar Khayyam, translated from the Persian by L.P. Elwell-Sutton in *In Search of Omar Khayyam* by Ali Dashti (New York, 1971)

I had supposed that, having passed away
From self in concentration, I should blaze
A path to Thee, but ah! No creature may
Draw near thee, save Thy appointed ways.
I cannot longer live, Lord, without Thee;
Thy Hand is everywhere: I may not flee.

Some have desired through hope to come to Thee,
And Thou hast wrought in them their high design:
Lo! I have severed every thought from me,
And died to selfhood, that I might be Thine.
How long, my heart's Beloved? I am spent:
I can no more endure this banishment.

—Abu'l-Husayn al-Nuri, *A Treasury of Traditional Wisdom* presented by
Whitall N. Perry (Louisville, 1992)

As the Arab racer needs not the whip,
So you will not need to fear
When on your journey you have started.

When purified are your soul and body,
You will not fear the fires of hell.
Throw pure gold into the fire;
If it contains no alloy, what is there to burn?

—Shabistari, *The Secret Rose Garden of Sa'ad Ud Din Mahmud Shabistari*
translated by Florence Lederer (London, 1920)

Even God must die, if He wishes to live for thee:
How thinkest thou, without dying, to inherit His Life?

God, whose sweet bliss it is to dwell within our breast,
Comes then most readily when we our house have left.

—Angelus Silesius, *The Cherubinic Wanderer* translated by Maria Shrady
(New York, 1986)

The chosen angels and the blessed souls
of Heaven's citizens, on the first day
my lady passed away, surrounded her,
all full of wonder and of reverence.

"What light is this, and what unusual beauty,"
they said to one another, "for so lovely
a soul in all this time has never risen
out of the erring world to this high home."

She, happy to have changed her dwelling,
is equal to the most perfected souls,
meanwhile, from time to time, she turns to see

if I am following her, and seems to wait;
so all my thoughts and wishes strain to Heaven—
I hear her praying that I hurry up.

—Petrarch, *Selections from the Canzoniere and Other Works* translated by
Mark Musa (Oxford, 1985)

I go my way regretting those past times
I spent in loving something which was mortal
instead of soaring high, since I had wings
that might have taken me to higher levels.

You who see all my shameful, wicked errors,
King of all Heaven, invisible, immortal,
help this frail soul of mine for she has strayed,
and all her emptiness fill up with grace,

so that, having once lived in storms, at war,
I may now die in peace, in port; and if my stay
was vain, at least let my departure count.

Over that little life that still remains to me,
and at my death, deign that your hand be present:
You know You are the only hope I have.

> —Petrarch, *Selections from the Canzoniere and Other Works*
> translated by Mark Musa (Oxford, 1985)

What is our life? A play of passion,
Our mirth the music of division,
Our mothers wombs the tiring houses be,
Where we are dressed for this short comedy,
Heaven the judicious sharp spectator is,
That sits and marks still who doth act amiss,
Our graves that hide us from the searching sun,
Are like drawn curtains when the play is done,
Thus march we playing to our latest rest,
Only we die in earnest, that's no jest.

—Sir Walter Raleigh, *The New Oxford Book of English Verse* chosen and
edited by Helen Gardner (Oxford, 1991)

O Years! and Age! Farewell:
Behold I Go,
Where I do know
Infinity to dwell.

And these mine eyes shall see
All times, how they
Are lost i' th' Sea
Of vast Eternity.

Where never Moon shall sway
The Stars; but she,
And Night, shall be
Drown'd in one endless Day.

—Robert Herrick, *A Treasury of Traditional Wisdom* presented by Whitall
N. Perry (Louisville, 1992)

Death be not proud, though some have called thee
Mighty and dreadful, for, thou art not so,
For, those, whom thou think'st thou dost overthrow,
Die not, poor death, nor yet canst thou kill me;
From rest and sleep, which but thy pictures be,
Much pleasure, then from thee, much more must flow,
And soonest our best men with thee do go,
Rest of their bones, and souls delivery.
Thou art slave to Fate, chance, kings, and desperate men,
And dost with poison, war, and sickness dwell,
And poppy, or charms can make us sleep as well,
And better than thy stroke; why swell'st thou then?
One short sleep past, we wake eternally,
And death shall be no more, Death thou shalt die.

—John Donne, *The New Oxford Book of English Verse* chosen and edited
by Helen Gardner (Oxford, 1991)

When as Man's life, the light of human lust,
In sockets of his earthly lanthorn burns,
That all this glory unto ashes must,
And generation to corruption turns;
Then fond desires that only fear their end,
Do vainly wish for life, but to amend.

But when this life is from the body fled,
To see itself in that eternal Glass,
Where time doth end, and thoughts accuse the dead,
Where all to come, is one with all that was;
Then living men ask how he left his breath,
That while he lived never thought of death.

—Fulke Greville, Lord Brooke, *The Oxford Book of English Mystical Verse*
chosen by D.H.S. Nicholson and A.H.E. Lee (Oxford, 1917)

To his Watch, when he could not Sleep

Incessant minutes, whilst you move you tell
The time that tells our life, which though it run
Never so fast or far, your new begun
Short steps shall overtake; for though life well

May 'scape his own account, it shall not yours;
You are Death's auditors, that both divide
And sum what ere that life inspired endures
Past a beginning, and through you we bide

The doom of Fate, whose unrecalled Decree
You date, bring, execute; making what's new,
Ill and good, old, for as we die in you,
You die in Time, Time in Eternity.

—Edward, Lord Herbert of Cherbury, *The New Oxford Book of English
Verse* chosen and edited by Helen Gardner (Oxford, 1991)

The expense of spirit in a waste of shame
Is lust in action; and till action, lust
Is perjured, murderous, bloody, full of blame,
Savage, extreme, rude, cruel, not to trust;
Enjoyed no sooner but despised straight;
Past reason hunted; and no sooner had,
Past reason hated, as a swallowed bait,
On purpose laid to make the taker mad:
Mad in pursuit, and in possession so;
Had, having, and in quest to have, extreme;
A bliss in proof, and proved, a very woe;
Before, a joy proposed; behind, a dream.
All this the world well knows, yet none knows well
To shun the heaven that lead men to this hell.

—William Shakespeare, Sonnet 129, *Complete Works* edited by W.J. Craig
(Oxford, 1964)

The times are all so fearful!
The heart so full of cares!
To eyes that question tearful
The future spectral stares.

Wild terrors creep and hover
With foot so ghastly soft!
The soul black midnights cover
Like mountains piled aloft.

Firm props like reeds are waving;
For trust is left no stay;
The thoughts, with whirlpool-raving,
No more the will obey.

Frenzy, with eye resistless,
Decoys from Truth's defense;
Life's pulse is flagging listless,
And dull is every sense.

Who hath the cross upheaved,
To shelter and make whole?
Who lives from sight received,
That he may help the soul?

Haste to the tree of wonder;
Give silent longing room;
Outgoing flames asunder
Will cleave the phantom-gloom.

Draws thee an angel tender
In safety on the strand;

Lo! At thy feet in splendor,
Outspreads the promised land.

> —Novalis, translated by George McDonald in *The Devotional Songs of Novalis* collected and edited by Bernhard Pick (London, 1910)

Self-Knowledge

Know yourself—and is this the prime
And heaven-sprung adage of the olden time?—
Say, canst thou make thyself?—Learn first that trade;—
Haply thou mayst know what thyself had made.
What hast thou, Man, that thou dar'st call thine own?—
What is there in thee, Man, that can be known?—
Dark fluxion, all unfixable by thought,
A phantom dim of past and future wrought,
Vain sister of the worm,—life, death, soul, clod—
Ignore thyself, and strive to know thy God!

—Samuel Taylor Coleridge, *The Complete Poems* edited by
William Keach (London, 1997)

Uphill

Does the road wind uphill all the way?
Yes, to the very end.
Will the day's journey take the whole long day?
From morn to night, my friend.

But is there for the night a resting-place?
A roof for when the slow, dark hours begin.
May not the darkness hide it from my face?
You cannot miss that inn.

Shall I meet other wayfarers at night?
Those who have gone before.
Then must I knock, or call when just in sight?
They will not keep you standing at that door.

Shall I find comfort, travel-sore and weak?
Of labor you shall find the sum.
Will there be beds for me and all who seek?
Yea, beds for all who come.

—Christina Georgina Rossetti, *The New Oxford Book of English Verse*
chosen and edited by Helen Gardner (Oxford, 1991)

Because I Could not Stop for Death

Because I could not stop for Death,
He kindly stopped for me;
The carriage held but just ourselves
And Immortality.

We slowly drove, he knew no haste,
And I had put away
My labor, and my leisure too,
For his civility.

We passed the school where children played
At wrestling in a ring;
We passed the fields of gazing grain,
We passed the setting sun.

We paused before a house that seemed
A swelling of the ground;
The roof was scarcely visible,
The cornice but a mound.

Since then 'tis centuries, but each
Feels shorter than the day
I first surmised the horses' heads
Were toward eternity.

—Emily Dickinson, *A Pocket Book of Modern Verse* edited by
Oscar Williams (New York, 1965)

Autumn

The leaves are falling, falling as from way off,
as though far gardens withered in the skies;
they are falling with denying gestures.

And in the night the heavy earth is falling
from all the stars down into loneliness.

We all are falling. This hand falls.
And look at others: it is in them all.

And yet there is one who holds this falling
endlessly gently in his hands.

—Rainer Maria Rilke, *Translations from the Poetry of Rainer Maria Rilke*
translated by M.D. Herter Norton (New York, 1993)

The Island

Islands of bliss and everlasting youth,
Floating like flowers on an endless sea
And never touched by sorrows from this world:
Such happy islands thou wilt never see.

Behold: what thou hast dreamt of may be real,
It is not elsewhere, it is what thou art
If thou rememb'rest God; then thou wilt find
The golden island in thy deepest heart.

The singing of a flute came from the sea;
The waters vanished, and the flute was me.

—Frithjof Schuon, *Road to the Heart* (Bloomington, 1995)

Confession

She that I sing of is the fairest day;
I that do sing am the profoundest death.
Like lightning am I, and my Word is wine;
The world lies deep within my heart's own beat.

Thou that seekest for the Singer, ask
Neither for name, nor yet for mine and thine;
For Love is all that the world-sea contains,
And death in Love of Love the essence is.

—Frithjof Schuon, translated by Barbara Perry in *The Essential Writings
of Frithjof Schuon* edited by Seyyed Hossein Nasr (New York, 1986)

Part II

A
Garden
Amidst
Flames

O marvel! A garden amidst flames!
My heart has become capable of every form:
it is a pasture for gazelles, and a convent for Christian monks,
And a temple for idols, and the pilgrim's Ka'ba,
and the tables of the Torah and the book of the Quran.
I follow the religion of Love: whatever way
Love's camels take, that is my religion and my faith.

—Ibn 'Arabi, *Tarjuman Al-Ashwaq: A Collection of Mystical Odes* translated
by Reynold A. Nicholson (London, 1911)

Layla

Full near I came unto where dwelleth
Layla, when I heard her call.
That voice, would I might ever hear it!
She favored me, and drew me to her,
Took me in, into her precinct,
With discourse intimate addressed me.
She sat me by her, then came closer,
Raised the cloak that hid her from me,
Made me marvel to distraction,
Bewildered me with all her beauty.
She took me and amazed me,
And hid me in her inmost self,
Until I thought that she was I,
And my life she took as ransom.
She changed me and transfigured me,
And marked me with her special sign,
Pressed me to her, put me from her,
Named me as she is named.
Having slain and crumbled me,
She steeped the fragments in her blood.
Then, after my death, she raised me:
My star shines in her firmament.
Where is my life, and where my body,
Where my willful soul? From her
The truth of these shone out to me
Secrets that had been hidden from me.
Mine eyes have never seen but her:
To naught else can they testify.
All meanings in her are comprised.
Glory be to her Creator!

Thou that beauty wouldst describe,
Here is something of her brightness
Take it from me. It is my art.
Think it not idle vanity.
My Heart lied not when it divulged
The secret of my meeting her.
If nearness unto her effaceth,
I still subsist in her subsistence.

—Ahmad al-'Alawi, *A Sufi Saint of the Twentieth Century* by Martin Lings
(Cambridge, UK, 1993)

The secret longings of a learned man
Are more mysterious than the fabled Phoenix;
Within the oyster grows a hidden pearl
From the deep longings of the boundless sea.

—Omar Khayyam, translated from the Persian by L.P. Elwell-Sutton in *In Search of Omar Khayyam* by Ali Dashti (New York, 1971)

A man knocked at the door of his beloved.
"Who are you, trusted one?" thus asked the friend.
He answered: "I!" The friend said: "Go away,
Here is no place for people raw and crude!"
What, then, could cook the raw and rescue him
But separation's fire and exile's flame?
The poor man went to travel a whole year
And burned in separation from his friend,
And he matured, was cooked and burnt, returned
And carefully approached the friend's abode.
He walked around it now in cautious fear
Lest from his lips unfitting words appear.
His friend called out: "Who is there at my door?"
The answer: "You, dear, *you* are at the door!"
He said: "Come in, now that you are all I—
There is no room in this house for two 'I's!"

—Rumi, *I Am Wind, You Are Fire: The Life and Work of Rumi* by Annemarie
Schimmel (Boston, 1992)

The Song of the Reed

Hearken to this Reed forlorn,
Breathing, even since 'twas torn
From its rushy bed, a strain
Of impassioned love and pain.

"The secret of my song, though near,
None can see and none can hear.
Oh, for a friend to know the sign
And mingle all his soul with mine!

'Tis the flame of Love that fired me,
'Tis the wine of Love inspired me,
Wouldst thou learn how lovers bleed,
Hearken, hearken to the Reed!"

—Rumi, *Rumi: Poet and Mystic* translated by Reynold A. Nicholson
(London, 1950)

The Unseen Power

We are the flute, our music is all Thine;
We are the mountains echoing only Thee;
Pieces of chess Thou marshallest in line
And movest to defeat or victory;
Lions emblazoned high on flags unfurled—
Thy invisible wind sweeps us through the world.

—Rumi, *Rumi: Poet and Mystic* translated by Reynold A. Nicholson
(London, 1950)

And this is love—
The vertigo of Heaven
Beyond the cage of words,
Suddenly to be naked
In the searchlight of truth ...

—Rumi, *Words of Paradise: Selected Poems of Rumi* translated by Rafieq
Abdulla (London, 2000)

Whatever I say, You are the subject.
Wherever I go, every impulse is toward You.

It's true, those who don't love You are soul-less dolls,
but the living need a Beloved like You.

You've veiled Yourself from the whole universe.
At a single sight of You it would perish.

Giants and elves, humans, angelic powers,
all beings are in love with You.

The seraphim and maidens of paradise crowd around You
and can't bear to leave Your presence.

From Your hand poison is a delicious drink.
My soul is healed by anything You do.

When I eat something sweet without You, it's bitter.
You are the soul's taste, what else could I want?

If my soul suffered a hundred wounds,
my joy would not decrease.
This love washes everything clean.

Yunus is just one atom of it. This planet,
this whole universe is born from a taste of love.

—Yunus Emre, *The Drop that Became the Sea: Lyric Poems of Yunus Emre*
translated by Kabir Helminski and Refik Algan (Putney, 1989)

Do you know, my friends, where the real saints are?
Wherever I look, wherever I want them, they're there.

My words bounce off the loveless like an echo from stone.
Do you know, whoever hasn't got at least an atom of love,
lives in a wilderness?

Don't be a liar, don't lie to love.
Whoever lies here, earns a sentence in the other world.

Oh, you unaware of Yourself,
you don't understand the meaning of words,
if you desire the realness of Truth,
here it is in knowledge and in the Quran:

If Allah says, "He is Mine,"
Allah keeps giving the realness of Love.
Whoever has an atom of Love,
has the realness of God within.

Many people tell Yunus,
"You're too old to be a lover,"
but this love is so new and fresh.

—Yunus Emre, *The Drop that Became the Sea: Lyric Poems of Yunus Emre*
translated by Kabir Helminski and Refik Algan (Putney, 1989)

Let the deaf listen to the mute.
A soul is needed to understand them both.

Without listening we understood.
Without understanding we carried it out.

On this Way, the seeker's wealth is poverty.

We loved, we became lovers.
We were loved, we became the beloved.
When all is perishing moment by moment
Who has time to be bored?

God divided His people into seventy-two languages
And borders arose.

But poor Yunus fills the earth and sky,
and under every stone hides a Moses.

—Yunus Emre, *The Drop that Became the Sea: Lyric Poems of Yunus Emre*
translated by Kabir Helminski and Refik Algan (Putney, 1989)

Lady, rise and offer to the Name,
Bearing in thy hand the flesh and wine.
Such shall never bring thee loss and shame,
Be it of no custom that is thine.

This they know for Knowledge that have found—
Be the loud Cry from His Place but heard—
Unity betwixt the Lord and Sound,
Just as Sound hath unison with Word.

—Lalla Yogishwari, *The Word of Lalla* by Sir Richard Temple
(Cambridge, UK, 1924)

"Think not on the things that are without:
fix upon thy inner Self thy Thought:
So shalt thou be freed from let or doubt":—
Precepts these that my Preceptor taught.

Dance then, Lalla, clothed but by the air:
Sing then, Lalla, clad but in the sky.
Air and sky: what garment is more fair?
"Cloth," saith Custom—Doth that sanctify?

—Lalla Yogishwari, *The Word of Lalla* by Sir Richard Temple
(Cambridge, UK, 1924)

He who utters the name of Shiva
Hundreds and hundreds of times
Grows great through the showering
Of the sweet, sublime nectar.
The marvelous power of this word
Enters even into the hearts of fools.

This word, which flows like honey
From the nectar-crescent of the moon,
Causes the highest nectar to flow—
This is the sound of Shiva. The blessed
Ever have this sound upon their lips.

—Utpaladeva, *Shaiva Devotional Songs of Kashmir: A Translation and Study of Utpaladeva's Shivastrotravali* by Constantina Rhodes Bailly (Albany, 1987)

Yogin, don't go—
at your feet a slave girl has fallen.
She lost herself
on the devious path of romance and
worship,
no one to guide her.
Now she's built
an incense and sandalwood pyre
and begs you to light it.
Dark One, don't go—
when only cinder remains,
rub my ash over your body.
Mira asked: Dark One,
can flame twist upon flame?

—Mirabai, *For Love of the Dark One: Songs of Mirabai* translated by Andrew
Schelling (Boston, 1993)

Binding my ankles with silver
I danced—
people in town called me crazy.
She'll ruin the clan
said my mother-in-law,
and the prince
had a cup of venom delivered.
I laughed as I drank it.
Can't they see?—
body and mind aren't something to lose,
the Dark One's already seized them.
Mira's lord can lift mountains,
He is her refuge.

—Mirabai, *For Love of the Dark One: Songs of Mirabai* translated by Andrew
Schelling (Boston, 1993)

God of the silent soul
  Awake, alone,
Today I will open a door
  And be known.

Whom do I seek all day
  In the swift outside?
I will learn the holy word
  Of eventide.

I light the lamp of my life
  With your life's light.
O priest, in quiet I will make
  My gift tonight.

Where the cosmos has taught
  A world to pray,
I too of that radiance
  Will hold a ray.

—Rabindranath Tagore, *Song Offerings* translated by Joe Winter
(London, 2000)

On a dark night
When Love burned bright
Consuming all my care,
While my house slept,
Unseen, I crept
Along the secret stair.

O blessed chance!
No human glance
My secret steps detected.
While my house slept,
I silent crept
In shadow well protected.

That blessed night
Concealed from sight,
Unseeing did I go,
No light to guide
But that inside
My eager heart aglow.

A guide as bright
As noonday light,
Which brought me where he dwelt,
Where none but he
Could wait for me
And make his presence felt.

Sweeter that night
Than morning light,
For Love did loving meet,
I knew him well,

And we could dwell
In ecstasy complete.

I gave him there
My thought, my care,
So did my spirit flower.
Love lay at rest
Upon my breast
That cedar-scented hour.

When morning air
Ruffled his hair
From off the ramparts blowing,
I felt his hand
A quiet command
Tranquility bestowing.

Then face to face
With Love's own grace,
My fears no more parading,
I left them there
With all my care
Among the lilies fading.

—St. John of the Cross, *The Poems of St John of the Cross* translated by
Kathleen Jones (Westminster, 1993)

I cannot dance O Lord, unless Thou lead me.
If Thou wilt that I leap joyfully
Then must Thou Thyself dance and sing!
Then will I leap for love—
From love to knowledge,
From knowledge to fruition,
From fruition to beyond all human sense.
There will I remain
And circle evermore.

—Mechthild of Magdeburg, *A Treasury of Traditional Wisdom* presented by
Whitall N. Perry (Louisville, 1992)

Ah! God-loving soul! In thy struggles
Thou art armed with measureless might,
And with so great a power of soul
That all the peoples of the world,
All the charm of thine own body,
All the legions of the devil,
All the powers of Hell—
Cannot separate thee from God.

—Mechthild of Magdeburg, *A Treasury of Traditional Wisdom* presented by
Whitall N. Perry (Louisville, 1992)

As I rode out one day not long ago
By narrow roads, and heavy with the thought
Of what compelled my going, I met Love
In pilgrim's rags coming the other way.
All his appearance seemed to speak such grief
As kings might feel upon the loss of crown;
And ever sighing, bent with thought he came,
His eyes averted from all passers-by.
Yet as we met he called to me by name
And said to me, "I come from that far land,
Where I had sent your heart to serve my will;
I bring it back to court a new delight."
And then so much of him was fused with me,
He vanished from my sight, I know not how.

—Dante Alighieri, *La Vita Nuova* translated by Mark Musa
(Bloomington, 1962)

Canticle of the Sun

Be thou praised, my Lord,
With all Thy creatures, above all Brother Sun,
Who gives the day and lightens us therewith.

And he is beautiful, and radiant with great splendor,
Of Thee, Most High, he bears similitude.

Be Thou praised, my Lord, of Sister Moon,
And the stars, in heaven Thou formed them,
Clear, precious and lovely.

Be Thou praised, my Lord, of Brother Wind,
And of the air, and cloud, of fair and of all weather,
By which Thou givest to Thy creatures sustenance.

Be Thou praised, my Lord, of Sister Water,
Humble, much useful, precious and pure.

Be Thou praised, my Lord, of Brother Fire,
By which Thou hast lightened the night,
And he is beautiful and joyful, robust and strong.

Be Thou praised, my Lord, of Sister Mother Earth,
Which sustains and hath us in her rule,
And produces diverse fruits, colored flowers and herbs.

Be Thou praised, my Lord, of those who pardon for Thy love
And endure sickness and tribulations.

Blessed are they who endure it in peace,
For by Thee, Most High, they shall be crowned.
Be Thou praised, my Lord, for Sister Death,

From whom no living man escapes;
And woe to those who die in mortal sin.

Blessed are they who are found in Thy holy will,
For the moment death shall work in them no ill.

Praise ye and bless my Lord, and give Him thanks,
And serve Him with a great humility.

—St. Francis of Assisi, *The Mirror of Perfection* translated by Robert
Steele (New York, 1963)

Love and the noble heart are but one thing,
Even as the wise man tells us in his rhyme,
The one without the other venturing
As well as reason from a reasoning mind.
Nature, disposed to love, creates Love king,
Making the heart a dwelling place for him
Wherein he lies quiescent, slumbering
Sometimes a little, now a longer time.
Then beauty in a virtuous woman's face
Pleases the eyes, striking the heart so deep
A yearning for the pleasing thing may rise.
Sometimes so long it lingers in that place
Love's spirit is awakened from his sleep.
By a worthy man a woman's moved likewise.

—Dante Alighieri, *La Vita Nuova* translated by Barbara Reynolds
(New York, 1969)

With rejoicing mouth,
with rejoicing tongue,
by day
and tonight
you will call.
Fasting, you will sing
with the voice of the lark
and perhaps
in our happiness,
in our delight,
from some place in the world,
the creator of man,
the Lord All-powerful,
will hear you.
"Ay!" he will say to you,
and you
wherever you are
and thus forever
with no other lord but him
will live, will be.

—Inca, *In the Trail of the Wind: American Indian Poems and Ritual Orations*
by John Bierhorst (New York, 1992)

That our earth mother may wrap herself
In a fourfold robe of white meal;
That she may be covered with frost flowers;
That yonder on all the mossy mountains
The forests may huddle together with the cold;
That their arms may be broken by the snow,
In order that the land may be thus,
I have made my prayer sticks into living beings.

—Zuni, *American Indian Poetry: An Anthology of Songs and Chants* edited by
George W. Cronyn (New York, 1962)

ℐ Pass the Pipe

Friend of Wakinyan,
I pass the pipe to you first.
Circling I pass to you who dwell with the Father.
Circling pass to beginning day.
Circling pass to the beautiful one.
Circling I complete the four quarters and the time.
I pass the pipe to the Father with the Sky.
I smoke with the Great Spirit.
Let us have a blue day.

—Sioux, *The Magic World: American Indian Songs and Poems* selected and
edited by William Brandon (New York, 1971)

O Saichi, where is the Land of Bliss?
My Land of Bliss is right here.
Where is the line of divisions?
Between this world and the Land of Bliss?
The eyes are the line of division.

—Saichi, *River of Fire, River of Water: An Introduction to the Pure Land Tradition of Shin Buddhism* by Taitetsu Unno (New York, 1998)

Wind and air are two,
But it is one wind, one air.
Amida and I are two,
But the compassion of Namu-amida-butsu* is one.

—Saichi, *River of Fire, River of Water: An Introduction to the Pure Land Tradition of Shin Buddhism* by Taitetsu Unno (New York, 1998)

*Editor's note: the *nembutsu*, "namu-amida-butsu" (I entrust myself to Amida Buddha) is the recitative prayer of the Pure Land tradition of Shin Buddhism. It has parallels in the "Jesus Prayer" of Orthodox Christianity, the Dhikr of Sufism and the Japa-Yoga of Hinduism.

I am a happy man, indeed!
I visit the Pure Land as often as I like:
I'm there and I'm back,
I'm there and I'm back,
I'm there and I'm back,
"Namu-amida-butsu! Namu-amida-butsu!"

—Saichi, *A Treasury of Traditional Wisdom* presented by Whitall N. Perry
(Louisville, 1992)

Among all living things—
Mountains and rivers,
Grasses and trees,
Even the sounds of
Blowing winds
And rising waves—
There is nothing
That is not *nembutsu*.

—Ippen, *The Record of Ippen* translated by Dennis Hirota (Kyoto, 1986)

The Buddha, in the causal stage, made the universal vow:
When beings hear my Name and think on me,
I will come to welcome each of them,
Not discriminating at all between the poor and the rich and
    well-born,
Not discriminating between the inferior and highly gifted,
Not choosing the learned and those upholding pure
    precepts,
Nor rejecting those who break precepts and whose evil
    karma is profound.
Solely making beings turn about and abundantly say the
    nembutsu,
I can make bits of rubble change into gold!

—Tz'u-min, *Shin Buddhism: Bits of Rubble Turn into Gold* by Taitetsu
Unno (New York, 2002)

Amidst the notes
Of my koto is another
Deep mysterious tone,
A sound that comes from
Within my own breast.

—Yosano Akiko, *One Hundred More Poems from the Japanese* translated by
Kenneth Rexroth (New York, 1974)

If you're looking for a place to rest,
Cold Mountain is good for a long stay.
The breeze blowing through the dark pines
Sounds better the closer you come.
And under the trees a white-haired man
Mumbles over his Taoist texts.
Ten years now he hasn't gone home;
He's even forgotten the road he came by.

—Han Shan, *Cold Mountain: 100 Poems by the T'ang Poet Han Shan*
translated by Burton Watson (New York, 1970)

Where gather mists and clouds, a happy world.
Thick swirls of incense smoke wreathe Heaven's Gate.
The bell of Prajna chimes through vacant days.
Amida's sutras are one on quiet nights—
Brooks sigh and sing like harps when rain has stopped.
Birds chirp sweet melodies as sunshine dims.
The Way lies not far off—why toil for it?
Bodhi bears fruit right here inside the heart.

—Huynh Sanh Thong, *An Anthology of Vietnamese Poems from the Eleventh through the Twentieth Centuries* (New Haven/London, 1996)

Today
My life is mirrored in
A morning glory.

—Moritake, *Japanese Death Poems: Written by Zen Monks and Haiku Poets on the Verge of Death* by Yoel Hoffman (Rutland, 1986)

Love

Love bade me welcome: yet my soul drew back,
Guilty of dust and sin,
But quick-eyed Love, observing me grow slack
From my first entrance in,
Drew nearer to me, sweetly questioning,
If I lacked anything.

"A guest," I answered, "worthy to be here."
Love said, "You shall be he."
"I, the unkind, ungrateful? Ah, my dear,
I cannot look on thee."
Love took my hand, and smiling did reply,
"Who made the eyes but I?"

"Truth, Lord, but I have marred them; let my shame
Go where it doth deserve."
"And know you not," says Love, "who bore the blame?"
"My dear, then I will serve."
"You must sit down," says Love, "and taste my meat."
So I did sit and eat.

—George Herbert, *The New Oxford Book of English Verse* chosen and
edited by Helen Gardner (Oxford, 1972)

Prayer

Prayer, the Church's banquet, Angels' age,
God's breath in man returning to his birth,
The soul in paraphrase, heart in pilgrimage,
The Christian plummet sounding heaven and earth;

Engine against the Almighty, sinner's tower,
Reversèd thunder, Christ-side-piercing spear,
The six-days' world transposing in an hour,
A kind of tune, which all things hear and fear;

Softness, and peace, and joy, and love, and bliss,
Exalted manna, gladness of the best,
Heaven in ordinary, man well drest,
The milky way, the bird of Paradise,

Church-bells beyond the stars heard, the soul's blood,
The land of spices; something understood.

—George Herbert, *The New Oxford Book of English Verse* chosen and
edited by Helen Gardner (Oxford, 1972)

Batter my heart, three-personed God, for you
As yet but knock, breathe, shine, and seek to mend;
That I may rise, and stand, overthrow me, and bend
Your force, to break, blow, burn and make me new.
I, like an usurped town, to another due,
Labor to admit you, but O, to no end.
Reason, your viceroy in me, me should defend,
But is captived and proves weak or untrue.
Yet dearly I love you and would be loved fain,
But am betrothed unto your enemy.
Divorce me, untie, or break that knot again,
Take me to you, imprison me, for I,
Except you enthrall me, never shall be free,
Nor ever chaste, except you ravish me.

—John Donne, *A Treasury of Traditional Wisdom* presented by Whitall N.
Perry (Louisville, 1992)

Lord, I am like to Mistletoe,
Which has no root, and cannot grow,
Or prosper, but by that same tree
It clings about; so I by Thee.

—Robert Herrick, *A Treasury of Traditional Wisdom* presented by Whitall
N. Perry (Louisville, 1992)

The lines of life are various; they diverge and cease
Like the footpaths and the mountains' utmost ends.
What here we are, elsewhere a God amends
With harmonies, eternal recompense and peace.

—Friedrich Hölderlin, translated by Michael Hamburger in *Selected Poems and Fragments* edited by Jeremy Adler (London, 1998)

The Divine Image

To Mercy, Pity, Peace and Love
All pray in their distress;
And to these virtues of delight
Return their thankfulness.

For Mercy, Pity, Peace and Love
Is God, our Father dear,
And Mercy, Pity, Peace and Love
Is man, His child and care.

For Mercy has a human heart,
Pity a human face,
And Love, the human form divine,
And Peace, the human dress.

Then every man, of every clime,
That prays in his distress,
Prays to the human form divine,
Love, Mercy, Pity and Peace.

And all must love the human form,
In heathen, Turk or Jew;
Where Mercy, Love, and Pity dwell
There God is dwelling too.

—William Blake, *The New Oxford Book of English Verse* chosen and edited
by Helen Gardner (Oxford, 1972)

When in hours of fear and failing,
All but quite our heart despairs;
When, with sickness driven wailing,
Anguish at our bosom tears;
When our loved ones we remember;
All their grief and trouble rue;
And their clouds of our December
Let no beam of hope shine through;

Then, oh then! God bends him o'er us;
Then his love grows very clear;
Long we heavenward then—before us
Lo, his angel standing near!
Fresh the cup of life he reaches;
Whispers courage, comfort new;
Nor in vain our prayer beseeches
Rest for the beloved too.

—Novalis, translated by George McDonald in *The Devotional Songs of
Novalis* collected and edited by Bernhard Pick (London, 1910)

Love's Lord

When weight of all the garner'd years
Bows me, and praise must find relief
In harvest-song, and smiles and tears
Twist in the band that binds my sheaf;

Thou known Unknown, dark, radiant sea
In whom we live, in whom we move,
My spirit must love itself in Thee,
Crying a name—Life, Light, or Love.

—Edward Dowden, *The Oxford Book of English Mystical Verse* chosen by
D.H.S. Nicholson and A.H.E. Lee (Oxford, 1917)

All in all

We know Thee, each in part—
A portion small;
But love Thee, as Thou art—
The All in all:
For Reason and the rays thereof
Are starlight to the noon of Love.

—John Bannister Tabb, *The Oxford Book of English Mystical Verse* chosen by
D.H.S. Nicholson and A.H.E. Lee (Oxford, 1917)

He who Knows Love

He who knows Love—becomes Love, and his eyes
Behold Love in the heart of everyone,
Even the loveless: as the light of the sun
Is one with all it touches. He is wise
With undivided wisdom, for he lies
In Wisdom's arms. His wanderings are done,
For he has found the Source whence all things run—
The guerdon of the quest, that satisfies.

He who knows Love becomes Love, and he knows
All beings are himself, twin-born of Love.
Melted in Love's own fire, his spirit flows
Into all earthly forms, below, above;
He is the breath and glamour of the rose,
He is the benediction of the dove.

—Elsa Barker, *The Oxford Book of English Mystical Verse* chosen by D.H.S.
Nicholson and A.H.E. Lee (Oxford, 1917)

The Name

Thy Name is wine and honey, melody
That shapes our sacred way and destiny.
Who is the Speaker and who is the Word?
Where is the song Eternity has heard?

The liberating Word comes from the sky
Of Grace and Mercy; and we wonder why
Such gift can be; the truth is not so far:
Thy name is That which is, and what we are.

—Frithjof Schuon, *Road to the Heart* (Bloomington, 1995)

The Drink

Because the drink is of an earthly brand
The drinker's heart they do not understand.
Now, earthly beauty, to the wise, is more
Than just a sign; it is an open door.

They think the lover's pilgrimage will fail
Because he meets not Layla, but her veil.
They do not see that with the Angel's kiss
We drink the wine of everlasting Bliss.

—Frithjof Schuon, *Road to the Heart* (Bloomington, 1995)

Part III

The Single Light

This desert is the Good
That no foot ever trod,
Created meaning
Never went there:
That is; but nobody knows what.
It is here, It is there,
It is far, It is near,
It is deep, It is high,
Thus It is
Neither this nor that.

It is light, It is clearness,
It is darkness,
It is unnamed,
It is unknown,
Free from the beginning and the end,
That stands still,
Naked, without cloth.

—Meister Eckhart, English translation by Patrick Laude from *Maître
Eckhart: Le grain de sénevé* edited by Alain de Libera (Paris, 1996)

Of the heavenly things God has shown me
I can speak but a little word,
Not more than a honey-bee
Can carry away on its foot
From an overflowing jar.

—Mechthild of Magdeburg, *A Treasury of Traditional Wisdom* presented by
Whitall N. Perry (Louisville, 1992)

Eternal Wisdom builds:
I shall the palace be
When I in Wisdom rest
And Wisdom rests in me.

—Angelus Silesius, *The Cherubinic Wanderer* translated by Willard Trask
(New York, 1953)

Lift up the cup and bowl, my darling one,
Walk proudly through the garden by the stream;
For many a slender beauty Heaven has made
Into a hundred cups, a hundred bowls.

—Omar Khayyam, translated from the Persian by L.P. Elwell-Sutton in *In Search of Omar Khayyam* by Ali Dashti (New York, 1971)

'Tis light makes color visible: at night
Red, green, and russet vanish from thy sight.
So to thee light by darkness is made known:
All hid things by their contraries are shown.
Since God hath none, He, seeing all, denies
Himself eternally to mortal eyes.

From the dark jungle as a tiger bright,
Form from the viewless Spirit leaps to light.
When waves of thought from Wisdom's Sea profound
Arose, they clad themselves in speech and sound.
The lovely forms a fleeting sparkle gave,
Then fell and mingled with the falling wave.
So perish all things fair, to re-adorn
The Beauteous One whence all fair things were born.

—Rumi, *Rumi: Poet and Mystic* translated by Reynold A. Nicholson
(London, 1950)

'Twas a fair orchard, full of trees and fruit
And vines and greenery. A Sufi there
Sat with eyes closed, his head upon his knee,
Sunk deep in meditation mystical.
"Why," asked another, "dost thou not behold
These Signs of God the Merciful displayed
Around thee, which He bids us contemplate?"
"The signs," he answered, "I behold within;
Without is naught but symbols of the Signs."

What is all beauty in the world? The image
Like quivering boughs reflected in a stream,
Of that eternal Orchard which abides
Unwithered in the hearts of Perfect men.

—Rumi, *Rumi: Poet and Mystic* translated by Reynold A. Nicholson
(London, 1950)

Ask of all those who know:
this body's life, what is it?
Life is the power of God alone,
and the blood in our veins, what is it?

Thought is a mere handmaiden
and doubt is anxiety's ore.
Lamentations are love's raiments.
A lord on his throne, what is he?

God is One and out of nothing,
thank God, He created the world.
In truth, we do not exist:
dominions and wealth, what are they?

God has summoned us to witness
His world that He created,
but no world is ever without end
and Solomon's kingdoms, what are they?

Ask Yunus, disciple of Taptuk,
What he has learned of this world?
It cannot last forever
and what are you, what am I?

—Yunus Emre, *The Drop that Became the Sea: Lyric Poems of Yunus Emre*
translated by Kabir Helminski and Refik Algan (Putney, 1986)

On the narrow path of Truth,
On the Meridian line, He stands upright,
Throwing no shadow before or behind Him,
To the right hand or the left.

East and west His Qibla is cast,
Drowned in a blaze of radiant light.

—Shabistari, *The Secret Rose Garden of Sa'd ud-Din Mahmud Shabistari*
translated by Florence Lederer (London, 1920)

In Being's silver sea
Lustrous pearls of knowledge are washed up
On the shore of speech.
And dainty shells bring poems in their curving forms
To strew the beach with beauty.

Each wave that breaks in foaming arcs
Casts up a thousand royal pearls
That hold strange murmuring voices,
Gems of devotion, joy, and love.

Yet though a thousand waves
At every moment rise and fall,
Scattering pearls and shells,
Yet are there ever more and more to come,
Nor is that sea of Being less by one sheer drop.

—Shabistari, *The Secret Rose Garden of Sa'd ud-Din Mahmud Shabistari*
translated by Florence Lederer (London, 1920)

"I" and "you" are but the lattices,
In the niches of a lamp,
Through which the One Light shines.

Between heaven and earth;
Lift this veil and you will see
No longer the bonds of sects and creeds.

When "I" and "you" do not exist,
What is mosque, what is synagogue?
What is the Temple of Fire?

—Shabistari, *The Secret Rose Garden of Sa'd ud-Din Mahmud Shabistari*
translated by Florence Lederer (London, 1920)

Ponder on God's mercies,
But not on His essence.
For His works come forth from His essence,
Not His essence from His works.
His light shines on the whole universe,
Yet He Himself is hidden from the universe.

—Shabistari, *The Secret Rose Garden of Sa'd ud-Din Mahmud Shabistari*
translated by Florence Lederer (London, 1920)

Where I wander—You!
Where I ponder—You!
Only You everywhere, You, always You.
You, You, You.
When I am gladdened—You!
And when I am saddened—You!
Only You, everywhere You!
You, You, You.
Sky is You!
Earth is You!
You above! You below!
In every trend, at every end,
Only You, everywhere You!

—Levi Yitzchak of Berditchov, *The Way of the Jewish Mystics* edited by
Perle Besserman (Boston, 1994)

Hymn of Glory for the Sabbath

… I have not seen thee, yet I tell Thy praise,
Nor known Thee, yet I image forth Thy ways.

For by Thy seers' and servants' mystic speech
Thou didst Thy sov'ran splendor darkly teach,

And from the grandeur of Thy work they drew
The measure of Thy inner greatness, too.

They told of Thee, but not as Thou must be,
Since from Thy work they tried to body Thee.

To countless visions did their pictures run,
Behold through all the visions Thou art one.

—Judah He-Hasid, *An Anthology of Mediaeval Hebrew Literature* edited by
Abraham A. Millgram (Philadelphia, 1935)

Song to the Sun

Thou eye of the Great God
Thou eye of the God of Glory
Thou eye of the King of creation
Thou eye of the Light of the living
Pouring on us at each time
Pouring on us gently, generously
Glory to thee thou glorious sun
Glory to thee thou Face of the God of life.

—Ortha nan Gaidheal, *A Treasury of Traditional Wisdom* presented by
Whitall N. Perry (Louisville, 1992)

Dawn Song

The black turkey in the east spreads his tail
The tips of his beautiful tail are the white dawn

Boys are sent running to us from the dawn
They wear yellow shoes of sunbeams

They dance on streams of sunbeams

Girls are sent dancing to us from the rainbow
They wear shirts of yellow

They dance above us the dawn maidens

The sides of the mountains turn to green
The tops of the mountains turn to yellow

And now above us on the beautiful mountains it is dawn.

—Mescalero Apache, *The Magic World: American Indian Songs and Poems*
selected and edited by William Brandon (New York, 1971)

Song

And I think over again
My small adventures
When with a shore wind I drifted out
In my kayak
And thought I was in danger.
My fears,
Those I thought so big,
For all the vital things
I had to get and to reach.

And yet, there is only
One great thing,
The only thing:
To live to see in huts and on journeys
The great day that dawns,
And the light that fills the world.

—Eskimo, *In the Trail of the Wind: American Indian Poems and Ritual Orations* edited by John Bierhorst (New York, 1971)

In the beginning was God,
Today is God,
Tomorrow will be God.
Who can make an image of God?
He has no body.
He is the word which comes out of your mouth
That word! It is no more,
It is past, and still it lives!
So is God.

—Pygmy, *An African Prayer Book* edited by Desmond Tutu
(New York, 1995)

There in midnight water,
Waveless, windless,
The old boat's swamped
With moonlight.

—Dogen, *Zen Poems of China and Japan* by Lucien Stryk, Takashi Ikemoto
and Taigan Takayama (New York, 1973)

To what shall
I liken the world?
Moonlight, reflected
In dewdrops,
Shaken from a crane's bill.

—Dogen, *The Zen Poetry of Dogen: Verses from the Mountain of Eternal Peace*
by Steven Heine (Boston, 1997)

Attaining the heart
Of the sutra
The sounds of the
Bustling marketplace
Preach the Dharma.

—Dogen, *The Zen Poetry of Dogen: Verses from the Mountain of Eternal Peace*
by Steven Heine (Boston, 1997)

Not limited
By language,
It is ceaselessly expressed;
So, too, the way of letters
Can display but not exhaust it.

—Dogen, *The Zen Poetry of Dogen: Verses from the Mountain of Eternal Peace*
by Steven Heine (Boston, 1997)

At Kugami
In front of the Otono,
There stands a solitary pine tree,
Surely of many a generation:
How divinely dignified
It stands there!
In the morning
I pass by it:
In the evening
I stand underneath it,
And standing I gaze,
Never tired
Of this solitary pine!

—Ryokwan, *A Treasury of Traditional Wisdom* presented by Whitall N. Perry (Louisville, 1992)

Snow

Flowers of ice
hide the heavens
no more blue sky
a silver dust
buries all the fields
and sinks the green mountains
Once the sun
comes out on the one
mountaintop
even the cold
that pierces to the bone
is a joy.

—Muso Soseki, *Sun at Midnight: Poems and Sermons* translated by W.S.
Merwin and Soiku Shigematsu (San Francisco, 1989)

Spring Cliff

Everywhere
soft breeze warm sunshine
the same calm
even the withered trees
on the dark cliff
are blossoming
I tried to find
where Subhuti
meditates
but suddenly in the shadow
of mist and fog
the path split a thousand ways.

—Muso Soseki, *Sun at Midnight: Poems and Sermons* translated by W.S.
Merwin and Soiku Shigematsu (San Francisco, 1989)

The question clear, the answer deep,
Each particle, each instant a reality,
A bird call shrills through mountain dawn:
Look where the old master sits, a rock, in Zen.

—Sodo, *Zen Prayers, Sermons, Anecdotes, Interviews* translated by Lucien
Stryk and Takashi Ikemoto (New York, 1963)

For no reason it rains,
whispers of reality.
How lovely it sings,
drop by drop.
Sitting and lying I listen
with emptied mind.
I don't need ears,
I don't need rain.

—Chin'gak, *Anthology of Korean Literature from Early Times to the Nineteenth Century* compiled and edited by Peter H. Lee (Honolulu, 1981)

Full Moon

Isolate and full, the moon
Floats over the house by the river.
Into the night the cold water rushes away below the gate.
The bright gold spilled on the river is never still.
The brilliance of my quilt is greater than precious silk.
The circle without blemish.
The empty mountains without sound.
The moon hangs in the vacant, wide constellations.
Pine cones drop in the old garden.
The senna trees bloom.
The same clear glory extends for ten thousand miles.

—Tu Fu, *One Hundred Poems from the Chinese* by Kenneth Rexroth
(New York, 1971)

Only this
Nothing more
No need to dust
No need to sit.

—Feng Kan, *Chinese Zen Poems, What Hold Has This Mountain?* edited by
Larry Smith and Mei Hui Huang (Huron, 1998)

Flowers not flowers, fog not fog;
It comes at midnight, goes at dawn.
Arriving like a spring dream,
Leaving like the morning clouds—
No way to hold it.

—Pai-Chu-i, *Chinese Zen Poems, What Hold Has This Mountain?* edited by
Larry Smith and Mei Hui Huang (Huron, 1998)

One in All,
All in One—
If only this is realized,
No more worry about your not being perfect!

—Seng-ts'an, *A Treasury of Traditional Wisdom* presented by Whitall N.
Perry (Louisville, 1992)

Sweetness is in sugar, sugar is in sweetness!
Both sweetness and sugar are in the tongue!
The tongue is in the mind and the mind is in the tongue!
Both tongue and mind are in You, O God!

Fragrance is in flowers and flowers in fragrance!
Both fragrance and flowers are in the sense of smell!
Not even my breath is in my hands! Everything is in You!

—Kanakadasa, *Sacred Songs of India* by V.K. Subramanian
(New Delhi, 1996)

Are you in illusion or is illusion in you?
Are you in the body or is the body in you?

Is the temple in the open field?
Or is the open field in the temple?
Both temple and field are in the eyes.
The eye is in the mind,
The mind is in the eye!
Both eye and mind are in you, O God!

—Kanakadasa, *Sacred Songs of India* by V.K. Subramanian
(New Delhi, 1996)

The pot is a god.
The winnowing fan is a god.
The stone in the street is a god.
The comb is a god.
The bowstring is also a god.
The bushel is a god and the spouted cup is a god.

Gods, gods, there are so many
there's no place left for a foot.

There is only one god—
He is our Lord of the Meeting Rivers.

—Basavanna, *Speaking of Shiva* translated by A.K. Ramanujan
(Baltimore, 1967)

The river and its waves are one surf:
where is the difference between the river and its waves?
When the wave rises, it is the water;
and when it falls, it is the same water again. Tell me, Sir,
where is the distinction? Because it has been named a wave
shall it no longer be considered as water?

Within the Supreme Brahma, the worlds are being told
Like beads: look upon that rosary with the eyes of wisdom.

—Kabir, *Songs of Kabir* translated by Rabindranath Tagore
(New York, 1974)

I laugh when I hear
That the fish in the water is thirsty:
You do not see that the Real is in your home
And you wander from forest to forest listlessly!
Here is the truth! Go where you will,
To Benares or Mathura; if you do not find your soul
The world is unreal to you.

—Kabir, *Songs of Kabir* translated by Rabindranath Tagore
(New York, 1974)

If Allah lives in a mosque,
Who inhabits the rest of the world?
Hindus say that he lives in the idol;
Both deceive themselves.
O Allah-Ram, it is for you that I live.
O master, have mercy on me.

One says that Hari lives in the south,
And that Allah resides in the west:
Search for him in your heart, search for him in every heart.
There is his dwelling and his residence.

—Kabir (source unknown)

Everything is pervaded by God!
Everything is pervaded by God!
What can be spoken? What cannot be spoken?
What can be done? What cannot be done?
Everything is pervaded by God!
What should be learnt? What should not be learnt?
What should be worshipped? What should not be
    worshipped?
Everything is pervaded by God!
What should be understood? What should not be
    understood?
What should be enjoyed? What should not be enjoyed?
Everything is pervaded by God!
Everywhere, always meditate on the Supreme!
This is the means of liberation!

—Sadasiva Brahmendra, *Sacred Songs of India* by V.K. Subramanian
(New Delhi, 1996)

Lo! a Vision is before mine eyes,
Framed in a halo of thoughts that burn:
Up into the Heights, lo! I arise
Far above the cries of them that spurn.

Lo! upon the wings Thought, my steed,
Into the mists of the evening gold,
High, and higher, and higher I speed
Unto the Man, the Self I behold.

Truth hath covered the nude that is I;
Girt me about with a flaming sword;
Clad me in the ethereal sky,
Garment of the glory of the Lord.

—Lalla Yogishwari, *The Word of Lalla* translated by Sir Richard Temple
(Cambridge, UK, 1924)

In a crack in the garden wall a flower
Blooms, nameless, lowly and obscure.
"Shame on this weed!" the plants tell each other;
The sun rises and calls, "Are you well, brother?"

—Rabindranath Tagore, *Rabindranath Tagore: An Anthology* edited by
Krishna Dutta and Andrew Robinson (New York, 1997)

Conviction

Like the bright day that shines on humankind
And with a light of heavenly origin
All things obscure and various gathers in,
Is knowledge, deeply granted to the mind.

—Friedrich Hölderlin, translated by Michael Hamburger in *Selected Poems
and Fragments* edited by Jeremy Adler (London, 1998)

Brahma

If the red slayer think he slays,
Or if the slain think he is slain,
They know not well the subtle ways
I keep, and pass, and turn again.

Far or forgot to me is near;
Shadow and sunlight are the same;
The vanished gods to me appear;
And one to me are shame and fame.

They reckon ill who leave me out;
When they fly, I am the wings;
I am the doubter and the doubt,
And I the hymn the Brahmin sings.

The strong gods pine for my abode,
And pine in vain the sacred Seven;
But thou, meek lover of the good!
Find me, and turn thy back on heaven.

—Ralph Waldo Emerson, *The Selected Writings of Ralph Waldo Emerson*
edited by Brooks Atkinson (New York, 1950)

I never saw a moor,
I never saw the sea;
Yet know I how the heather looks,
And what a wave must be.

I never spoke with God,
Nor visited in heaven;
Yet certain am I of the spot
As if a chart were given.

—Emily Dickinson, *A Pocket Book of Modern Verse* edited by Oscar
Williams (New York, 1965)

Elevation

Above the valleys, over rills and meres,
Above the mountains, woods, the oceans, clouds,
Beyond the sun, past all ethereal bounds,
Beyond the borders of the starry spheres,
My agile spirit, how you take your flight!
Like a strong swimmer swooning on the sea
You gaily plough the vast immensity
With manly, inexpressible delight.
Fly far above this morbid, vaporous place;
Go cleanse yourself in higher, finer air,
And drink up, like a pure, divine liqueur,
Bright fire, out of clear and limpid space.
Beyond ennui, past troubles and ordeals
That load our dim existence with their weight,
Happy the strong-winged man, who makes the great
Leap upward to the bright and peaceful fields!
The man whose thoughts, like larks, take to their wings
Each morning, freely speeding through the air,
—Who soars above this life, interpreter
Of flowers' speech, the voice of silent things!

—Charles Baudelaire, *Flowers of Evil* translated by James McGowan
(Oxford, 1998)

The Quest

For years I sought the Many in the One,
I thought to find lost waves and broken rays,
The rainbow's faded colors in the sun—
The dawns and twilights of forgotten days.

But now I seek the One in every form,
Scorning no vision that a dewdrop holds,
The gentle Light that shines behind the storm,
The Dream that many a twilight hour enfolds.

—Eva Gore-Booth, *The Oxford Book of English Mystical Verse* chosen by
D.H.S. Nicholson and A.H.E. Lee (Oxford, 1917)

Lost and Found

I missed him when the sun began to bend;
I found him not when I had lost his rim;
With many tears I went in search of him,
Climbing high mountains which did still ascend,
And gave me echoes when I called my friend;
Through cities vast and charnel-houses grim,
And high cathedrals where the light was dim,
Through books and arts and works without end,
But found him not—the friend whom I had lost.
And yet I found him—as I found the lark,
A sound in field heard but could not mark;
I found him nearest when I missed him most;
I found him in my heart, a life in frost,
A light I knew not till my soul was dark.

—George MacDonald, *The Oxford Book of English Mystical Verse* chosen
by D.H.S. Nicholson and A.H.E. Lee (Oxford, 1917)

Immanence

They think the world is blooming, while the heart
Renouncing it for God is poor and dark;
In this abyss, they say, thou wilt not find
The golden Paradise thou hast in mind;
They see not that the mystery of night
Means Layla dancing in a globe of light.

The deepest heart contains the holy shrine,
The naked goddess and the cup of wine.

—Frithjof Schuon, *Road to the Heart* (Bloomington, 1995)

Maya

The Sovereign Good is real, the world is dream;
The dream-world has its roots in the Supreme,
Who cast His image in the endless sea
Of things that may be or that may not be.

The fabric of the Universe is made
Of rays and circles, or of light and shade;
It veils from us the Power's burning Face
And unveils Beauty and Its saving Grace.

—Frithjof Schuon, *Road to the Heart* (Bloomington, 1995)

The Song

A finite image of Infinity:
This is the purpose of all poetry.
All human work to its last limits tends;
Its Archetype in Heaven never ends.
What is the sense of Beauty and of Art?
To show the way into our inmost Heart—

To listen to the music of the Sky;
And then to realize: the Song was I.

—Frithjof Schuon, *Road to the Heart* (Bloomington, 1995)

BIOGRAPHICAL NOTES ON SELECTED POETS

(In order of appearance)

GIUN: a Japanese Zen monk who died on October 12, 1333. This is his death haiku.

KIGEN: a Japanese haiku poet who died on August 23, 1736 at the age of seventy-one.

KOZAN ICHIKYO: a Japanese Zen monk who died on February 12, 1360 at the age of seventy-seven. According to Yoel Hoffman, "A few days before his death, Kozan called his pupils together, ordered them to bury him without ceremony, and forbade them to hold services in his memory. He wrote this poem on the morning of his death, laid down his brush, and died sitting upright."

ISSA (1763–1827): renowned for his subjective and individualistic *haiku*, which often draw on local dialects and daily conversations; it has been said that "the majority of Japanese who like traditional *haiku* probably know and like Issa better than any other poet."

HAN SHAN (COLD MOUNTAIN): a 7th century Chinese Buddhist layman of the T'ang period who wrote many poems about his solitary hermit life on Mount Han-shan and became a celebrated figure in the Ch'an/Zen tradition. He and his friend Shih-te are renowned for their eccentric wisdom and their search for enlightenment.

RYOKAN (1758?–1831): a Japanese Zen monk of the Soto school who was ordained as a monk when only eighteen. His poetical expressions of Zen realization are among the most beautiful in Japanese literature.

RENGETSU: she was born as Otagaki Nobu in the pleasure quarters of Kyoto in 1791, the illegitimate daughter of a Samurai warrior and a young geisha. In her early thirties she left the world having suffered the deaths of two husbands and two infant children, whereafter she betook ordination as a Buddhist nun and was given the name Rengetsu (Lotus Moon). She was not only a *waka* poet, but also a calligrapher, potter and painter.

CHONG CH'OL: a Korean poet who was born in 1536. His involvement in the political tribulations of the day eventually led him to withdraw from public life. He composed his verse in the classical Korean poetical forms of *kasa* and *sijo*.

LALLA YOGESHWARI: the present-day Muslims of Kashmir continue to venerate Lalla—the 14th century dancing Shaivite—as they would a Muslim saint; Hindus share in this dual cult. The doctrine of the naked yogini of the valley is condensed in one of her songs: "My guru gave me but a single precept. He told me: 'From without, enter into the inmost place.' For me this has become a rule; and this is why, naked, I dance."

AKKA MAHADEVI: a 12th century celibate devotee of Shiva, who lived in the Karnataka, a region on the southwest coast of India, and who died very young. Her verse lyrics were written in the Kannada language.

TULSIDAS (1532–1623): regarded as the greatest Hindu poet of his time, he was abandoned at birth and raised by a monk. In later life, the wise but reproachful words of his beloved wife—"If you had half as much love for Rama as you do for this perishable body, all your sorrows would be over and you would realize enlightenment"—led him to renounce the world and consecrate his life exclusively to Rama. His translation of the epic *Ramayana* into Hindi is still today the most influential version in northern and central India.

MIRABAI (1498–1547): a princess-poet and saint-singer who was born into a royal family in Mewar, Rajasthan. From childhood she was a devotee of Krishna. Married young, and following the death of her husband, she began to live a God-oriented life of prayer and contemplation. Seeing herself as the bride of Krishna, she poured forth streams of ecstatic poetry which are still sung today throughout India.

RABINDRANATH TAGORE (1861–1941): the renowned Bengali poet received the Nobel Prize for Literature in 1913, primarily for his work *Gitanjali* (Song Offerings), from which the poems in this collection are chosen. Each poem of Tagore's is a clear and lyrical expression of the metaphysical insight of a great soul, whose best work many in India view as a kind of holy book.

YUNUS EMRE: popular Turkish bard of the 13th century whose poetry is prized for its ability to express highly intellectual concepts in the simple diction of everyday spoken Turkish. For centuries his poetry has been recited by both learned scholars and illiterate peasants. He is especially revered by members of the Kizilbash Dervish brotherhoods, who fomented a revolt against feudal tyranny; and by many of the village bards who delight in showing several "tombs" of the legendary bard to tourists.

ANSARI (1006–1089): a renowned Persian Sufi Master, scholar and poet.

RUMI (1207–1273): a revered Sufi Master and founder of the Turkish-based Mevlavi order of "whirling dervishes." He is one of the greatest spiritual poets of the Persian language—and certainly one of the greatest in any language. His vast body of poetry includes the lengthy epic, the *Mathnawi*, which for some takes on an importance second only to the Quran itself. He also wrote more than three thousand lyrics and odes, many of which came to him while he was in a state of mystical ecstasy.

OMAR KHAYYAM (1048–1131): Persian mathematician, astronomer and poetic master of metaphysical paradox. The *Rubaiyat of Omar Khayyam*, translated by Edward Fitzgerald in the 19th century, has become a classic of mystical literature.

ABU'L-HUSAYN AL-NURI (d. 907): a famous Sufi teacher at Baghdad.

SHABISTARI (b.c. 1250–1320): Sa'd ud-Din Mahmud Shabistari was one of the greatest Persian Sufi poets whose work *The Secret Rose Garden* is considered amongst the world's classics of mystical literature.

ANGELUS SILESIUS (1624–1677): Johann Scheffler was born to Protestant parents in the Silesian capital of Breslau, seven years after the Thirty Years' War began unsettling Europe. At the age of 29, after graduating from the University of Padua, he converted to Catholicism and took the name Angelus Silesius. His poetic work, *The Cherubinic Wanderer*, prolongs the line of Christian gnosis represented by Meister Eckhart and also incorporates ideas from the German Protestant "theosophist" Jacob Böhme.

PETRARCH (1304–1374): Italy's greatest lyric poet whose *Canzoniere* is a classic of world literature. In his sonnets the passion of worldly love combines with spiritual yearning to create some of the most beautiful poems known to humakind.

SIR WALTER RALEIGH (1552?–1618): Elizabethan courtier, navigator, historian and poet. Under sentence of death, he spent 12 years in the tower of London where he wrote his *History of the World*.

ROBERT HERRICK (1591–1674): English lyric and spiritual poet; vicar of Dean Prior.

JOHN DONNE (1572–1631): Anglican minister and the foremost member of the "metaphysical" school of poets, which included George Herbert, Richard Crashaw, Andrew Marvell, and Henry Vaughan, all of whom were influenced by Donne.

FULKE GREVILLE, LORD BROOKE (1554–1628): a friend of Sir Philip Sidney, Lord Brooke entertained Giordano Bruno during his visit to London in 1583. Apart from the unauthorized edition of his *Mustapha*, which appeared in 1609, his works were published posthumously.

EDWARD, LORD HERBERT OF CHERBURY (1583–1648): a friend of John Donne and Ben Jonson, Lord Herbert was knighted by James I and became ambassador to France. His principal work is *De Veritate*, which was published in 1624.

WILLIAM SHAKESPEARE (1564–1616): England's sovereign playwright and poet.

NOVALIS (1772–1801): the pen-name of the German romantic poet and visionary philosopher Friedrich von Hardenberg. His book *Hymns to the Night* was influenced by Hermetic philosophy, and he could write: "Since God was able to become man, he can become even stones, plants, animals and elements, and perhaps there is in this way a perpetual deliverance in nature."

SAMUEL TAYLOR COLERIDGE (1772–1834): the intellectually gifted son of a Devonshire parson-schoolmaster, he became a renowned Romantic poet and Christian Platonist, and was the author of such popular poems as *The Rime of the Ancient Mariner* and the alluring but incomplete *Kubla Khan*.

CHRISTINA GEORGINA ROSSETTI (1830–1894): a sister of the Pre-Raphaelite artist and poet Dante Gabriel Rossetti. Twice engaged to be married, both times she refused on account of her scruples as a devout member of the Anglican Church. Her life of stoicism is well reflected in her poems, which are noted for their clear-cut imagery, light, buoyant rhythm, and sincere pathos.

EMILY DICKINSON (1830–1886): living most of her life as a recluse in her family home in Amherst, Massachusetts, and dressing only in white, her poems were almost completely unknown during her lifetime. She is now widely considered to be one of the greatest of all American poets.

RAINER MARIA RILKE (1875–1926): considered by many as the greatest poet of the 20th century, Rilke's lyrical voice, descriptive powers and yearning for a life of beauty and inwardness touches the very soul of the human condition.

FRITHJOF SCHUON (1907–1998): best known as the 20th century's foremost expositor of the Perennial Philosophy, Schuon wrote more that 3,000 short poems during the last three years of his life. Although the vast majority of these poems were composed in his native German tongue, almost all of the selections in this volume are taken from around 100 poems he wrote in English.

IBN 'ARABI (1165–1240): one of the most profound figures in the history of world spirituality. Known as the "Greatest Master" in Sufi circles, he traveled widely in the Islamic world, and wrote upwards of 350 treatises on the mystical path. His work was dedicated to exposing, at the deepest level, the primordial Unity underlying all human and natural existence.

AHMAD AL-'ALAWI (1869–1934): an Algerian saint considered by many to be one of the greatest Sufi Masters of the 20th century. He was largely unknown in the West until the publication of

Martin Lings' classic work *A Sufi Saint of the Twentieth Century: the Spiritual Legacy of Shaykh Ahmad al-'Alawi*. The poem presented here was translated by Martin Lings.

UTPALADEVA (ca. 900–950): a master of the tantric tradition in Kashmir who was considered to be a *siddha*, a "perfected being." He is best known for his philosophical treatises, in particular the *Shivastrotravali*, which reflects his perspective of perceiving the divine in ordinary life.

ST. JOHN OF THE CROSS (1542–1591): a Spanish mystic whose poetry of love and joy describes the soul's passage through the "dark night" of veiling and separation, to its final illumination and union with God. The allegory of earthly love transformed is the same as that found in the Old Testament *Song of Songs*.

MECHTHILD OF MAGDEBURG (1210–1297): a German visionary and mystical poet who saw "all things in God and God in all things." The Latin translation of her book *The Flowing Light of the Godhead* is said to have influenced Dante. As a member of the Beguine order of lay sisters, she lived a life of charity, nursing and strict religious observance.

DANTE ALIGHIERI (1265–1321): one of the greatest poets in the history of the world. The sonnets chosen here are from his book *The New Life*, where the beloved lady Beatrice becomes the poet's guide to God. Allegorically, she assumes this role once more in Dante's masterwork *The Divine Comedy*.

ST. FRANCIS OF ASSISI (1182–1226): a medieval mystic and founder of the Franciscan order; one of the most beloved saints of the Catholic Church. Embracing a life of holy poverty, he was especially known for his love of nature and animals, preaching a famous sermon on gratitude to the birds.

SAICHI: a 19th century Japanese Pure Land Buddhist cobbler and unlettered poet, called by D.T. Suzuki "one of the deepest Shin followers."

IPPEN (1239–1289): a Buddhist monk who attained religious awakening through the Pure Land way and then spent the rest of his life in wandering. The poem in this collection is a summary of Ippen's view that everything in creation is saying the Name of Amida Buddha.

TZ'U-MIN: a Chinese Pure Land master of the 8th century

YOSANO AKIKO (1878–1942): the only truly great Japanese poet to write in the traditional *tanka* form in modern times. Her work has been compared to Christina Georgina Rossetti, Louise Labe and Gaspara Stampa. She also translated the voluminous *Tale of Genji* into modern Japanese.

MORITAKE (1452–1540): a priest and one of the leading Japanese poets of the 16th century. He was a distinguished *renga* poet who composed witty and humorous verses he called *haikai*, which later became synonymous with *haiku*.

GEORGE HERBERT (1593–1633): younger brother of Edward, Lord Herbert of Cherbury. Initially a lecturer in rhetoric at Cambridge, he later became an Anglican priest. Herbert opposed the secularization of poetry and consequently wrote no secular verse. In his first year at Cambridge he sent two sonnets to his mother, promising to consecrate his "poor abilities in poetry" to God's glory. His collected poems, entitled *The Temple*, were published just a few months after his death and were regularly reprinted through the century.

FRIEDRICH HÖLDERLIN (1770–1843): one of the greatest of the German lyric poets, who melded classical and Christian themes in his highly sensitive poetry; he shared the classicists' love of "noble simplicity and calm greatness," and added to this his mystical sense of nature along with elements drawn from Christianity.

WILLIAM BLAKE (1757–1827): thought to be all but mad during his lifetime, Blake is now considered as one of England's greatest Romantic poets and artists, as well as one of the earliest and most vociferous critics of the Industrial Revolution. Asked about the Divinity of Jesus Christ, Blake responded: "He is the only God, and so am I, and so are you."

EDWARD DOWDEN (1843–1913): renowned Irish literary critic, scholar, and poet.

JOHN BANNISTER TABB (1845–1909): Catholic priest, educator, and poet.

ELSA BARKER (1869–1954): American novelist, short story writer, and poetess.

MEISTER ECKHART (1260–1327): a German Dominican theologian, and foremost of the Rhenish contemplatives renowned for Christian gnosis. Ananda K. Coomaraswamy said of Eckhart that he resumes and concentrates "in one consistent demonstration the spiritual being of Europe at its highest tension."

LEVI YITZCHAK OF BERDITCHOV (1740–1810): one of the most beloved figures in Jewish history, who introduced Hassidism (Jewish mysticism) to Poland. He was a disciple of the Hassidic master Dov Baer, the Maggid of Mezhirech, himself the foremost disciple of the Baal Shem Tov. Rabbi Levi stressed the importance of joy (*devekut*, or adhesion to God), the necessity for fervent prayer, and the importance of looking for the good in other people.

JUDAH HE-HASID (1150–1217): a Rhenish rabbi from Regensburg in southern Germany; he was a member of the pietest Jewish circle known as the Hasidei Ashkenaz, and is the author of the *Sefer Hasidim* ("Book of the Pious"), a work which contains legends and aphorisms expressing Hassidic wisdom.

ORTHA NAN GAIDHEAL: translated as "Song of the Gaels," this is an ancient and little known text supplied to Whitall N. Perry for inclusion in his monumental compendium entitled *A Treasury of Traditional Wisdom*.

DOGEN (1200–1253): a Zen Master and founder of the Soto sect. According to Tanabe Hajime, one of the leading modern philosophers in Japan associated with the Kyoto School, "Dogen's *Shobogenzo* is matchless in its command of Japanese language and logic with the power to realize the ineffable in and through speech and discussion."

MUSO SOSEKI (1275–1351): a Zen Master and founder of what is now called the rock garden. Muso's use of poetry and his simple, attractive teachings were designed to appeal to an unlettered audience. Although suspicious of any involvement with literature, he realized that it was through his poetry that he could communicate Zen for the benefit of all people.

TU FU (712–790): for over a millennium the Chinese have almost unanimously considered Tu Fu to be their greatest poet. The wanderings of Tu Fu are evocative of the transient nature of the human condition itself. He was the first of the Chinese poets of the T'ang dynasty to embrace life-experience as a proper subject matter for poetry, and the depth of his empathy for the human condition is testimony of the greatness of his soul.

FENG KAN (7th century): a Chinese Ch'an (Zen) Master of the T'ang dynasty. He was abbot of the Kuo-ch'ing Monastery in the T'ien-t'ai Mountains.

PAI-CHU-I (772–846): a devout Buddhist and one of the most famous poets and men of letters of the T'ang period. He held several senior official posts, but his outspoken criticism of government policy resulted in his being exiled to Chang'an.

SENG-TS'AN (d. 606?): the Third Patriarch in the Ch'an (Zen) school of Chinese Buddhism whose enlightened mind embraced the insights of Taoism and Ch'an in a supreme metaphysical synthesis. "The venerable way (Tao) is not difficult at all," he wrote in a poem, "it only abhors picking and choosing."

KANAKADASA (16th century): devoted to Lord Krishna from his childhood, he was a bitter critic of the caste system. This theme comes out in his song *Kula Kula vennu*: "What is the caste of the soul? What is the caste of Life? When God who resides in the inner soul blesses, what caste is a caste?" He lived to 98 years of age and traveled through India singing the praises of God.

BASAVANNA (1106–1168): a spiritual master in Karnataka, India, who propagated moral, ethical, and spiritual values for the reformation of Indian society.

KABIR (1440–1518): born of Muslim parents, in early life he became a disciple of the celebrated Hindu ascetic Ramananda. He maintained that Brahman and the creature are "ever distinct, yet ever united"; and that the wise man knows the spiritual as well as the material world to "be no more than His footstool." His vision of God was utterly synthetic: for Kabir there existed only the sheerest of veils between the material and the spiritual world.

SADASIVA BRAHMENDRA (17th century): became a recluse from a young age and wandered from place to place totally naked and observing silence. Considered as a *jivanmukta* (one liberated in this life), he was of the non-dualist (*advaita*) lineage of Shankara; and like his great predecessor, he composed devotional songs in Sanskrit extolling the greatness of Krishna and Rama.

RALPH WALDO EMERSON (1803–1882): influential American poet and essayist; one of the leading figures among the New England Transcendentalists, who were enamoured of newly available Eastern metaphysical texts such as the Vedas, the Upanishads and the Bhagavad Gita. Emerson considered the Bhagavad Gita to be "the first of books" and the poem included here bears comparison with the words of Lord Krishna to Arjuna on the battlefield of Kurukshetra (2:19).

CHARLES BAUDELAIRE (1821–1867): a French poet, translator, and literary and art critic. In his often introspective poetry, Baudelaire revealed himself as a seeker of God without religious beliefs, searching in every manifestation of life for its true significance, be it in the leaves of a tree or a prostitute's frown. In the preface to his *Flowers of Evil*, he characterized poetry as an alchemical process through which the poet extracts the quintessential sap from phenomena, be they seemingly ugly or ordinary.

EVA GORE-BOOTH (1870–1928): third child of Sir Henry Gore-Booth, poetess, writer, feminist, suffragette and mystic. Reacting against her privileged background, she devoted much time to helping the poor and disadvantaged, working tirelessly to better the working conditions of women in England. In her later life she was forced to give up active work through ill-health and turned increasingly to the composition of mystical poetry.

GEORGE MACDONALD (1824–1905): a Scotsman who received a "calling" to become a minister of a chapel in Arundel, England in 1850. In 1852 he was accused of heresy for expressing belief in a future state of probation for "heathens" (i.e. members of other revealed religions). Thereafter he embarked upon a varied career, which included lecturing, tutoring, occasional preaching, and the writing of fantasy. He was called by G.K. Chesterton a "St. Francis of Aberdeen, seeing the same sort of halo round every flower and bird."

INDEX OF AUTHOR NAMES

INDEX OF TITLES AND FIRST LINES OF POEMS

(Poem titles appear in italics)

For a glossary of all key foreign words used in books published by World Wisdom,
including metaphysical terms in English, consult:
www.DictionaryofSpiritualTerms.org.
This on-line Dictionary of Spiritual Terms provides extensive definitions,
examples and related terms in other languages.

BIOGRAPHICAL NOTES ON THE EDITORS

PATRICK LAUDE is Professor of French at Georgetown University and the author of numerous articles, translations, and books on the relationship between mysticism, symbolism and literature. His works include studies of important spiritual figures such as Jeanne Guyon, Simone Weil, Louis Massignon, and Frithjof Schuon. His most recent book is *Singing the Way: Insights in Poetry and Spiritual Transformation*, forthcoming with World Wisdom in 2005.

BARRY McDONALD serves as Managing Director of World Wisdom Inc. A strong attraction to authentic spirituality led him to many parts of the world and brought him in contact with spiritual authorities from several traditions. Thomas Yellowtail, the venerable Medicine Man and Sun Dance Chief, adopted him into his Crow tribe. He is the editor of *Every Branch in Me: Essays on the Meaning of Man* (World Wisdom, 2002) and *Seeing God Everywhere: Essays on Nature and the Sacred* (World Wisdom, 2003); his poetry has appeared in *CrossCurrents*, *Sacred Web*, *Sophia*, and *Sufi*.

Titles in the Spiritual Classics Series by World Wisdom

The Buddha Eye: An Anthology of the Kyoto School and Its Contemporaries, edited by Frederick Franck, 2004

The Gospel of the Redman, compiled by Ernest Thompson Seton and Julia M. Seton, 2005

Lamp of Non-Dual Knowledge & Cream of Liberation: Two Jewels of Indian Wisdom by Sri Swami Karapatra and Swami Tandavaraya, translated by Swami Sri Ramanananda Saraswathi, 2003

Light on the Indian World: The Essential Writings of Charles Eastman (Ohiyesa), edited by Michael Oren Fitzgerald, 2002

Music of the Sky: An Anthology of Spiritual Poetry, selected and edited by Patrick Laude and Barry McDonald, 2004

The Mystics of Islam by Reynold A. Nicholson, 2002

Naturalness: A Classic of Shin Buddhism by Kenryo Kanamatsu, 2002

Tripura Rahasya: The Secret of the Supreme Goddess, translated by Swami Sri Ramanananda Saraswathi, 2002

The Way of Sufism by Titus Burckhardt, 2006